LOVE
IS THE SEED

Teachings from the Spirit World

LISA HROMADA

ARS METAPHYSICA

an imprint of Sunbury Press, Inc.
Mechanicsburg, PA USA

ARS METAPHYSICA

an imprint of Sunbury Press, Inc.
Mechanicsburg, PA USA

For information about special discounts for bulk purchases, please contact Sunbury Press Orders Dept. at (855) 338-8359 or orders@sunburypress.com.

To request one of our authors for speaking engagements or book signings, please contact Sunbury Press Publicity Dept. at publicity@sunburypress.com.

ISBN: 978-1-62006-167-1 (Trade paperback)

Library of Congress Control Number: Application in Process

FIRST ARS METAPHYSICA EDITION: August 2019

Product of the United States of America
0 1 1 2 3 5 8 13 21 34 55

Set in Bookman Old Style
Designed by Crystal Devine
Flower vector created by freepik (www.freepik.com)
Cover by Lisa Hromada
Edited by Lawrence Knorr

Continue the Enlightenment!

A FINAL UNDERSTANDING of love's truth lies
within each person's understanding on Earth
and each soul's understanding wherever.
For through free will one travels many
paths in pursuit of truth. When those about
you are not in agreement with what you know within,
then look within and ask for guidance,
it is there. Each soul, each person on Earth,
understands this at the core of its being.

—Jesus, Session: January 31, 1982 Session 105 Page 3

THESE TEACHINGS are dedicated
to all seekers who believe
that a greater force guides them
and who yearn to know more about it
and reconnect with the Love
from which they were created.

To my mother and father —
who were open and willing to help bring
these messages of love to the world
— thank you.

IN MEDITATION AND PRAYER,
we relax into the divine guiding centering
field of aware knowing that is beyond
thinking or emotions.
On the other side of that still guiding
silence within Knower Soul,
there are various enlightenments.

✽

Download free meditations, practices, prayers,
and other resources at
www.LoveIsTheSeed.com

CONTENTS

INTRODUCTION

Today is not an ordinary day, it is an extraordinary day. It is filled with more love than you can possibly fathom. The love is in every minute detail and every atom of creation. And it is this day, this moment, that is going to be the most meaningful. Why? Because you have chosen it, whether consciously or having been subconsciously guided to this moment, where your life calls you to discover new things to improve your life here and now as well as your own soul's growth in evolution. This book is just one resource to help you.

Love is the Seed: Teachings from the Spirit World offers you a perspective on the purpose of this life on Earth, your connection to divine love and the empowerment it is to have love, thought and free will as divine tools to help you, as soul, continually mature into higher levels of knowing and completeness. It has been incredibly helpful for me and my hope is the same for you.

When I decided to share these unedited sessions, my intention was and is to give you the opportunity to find your own personal meaning and uncover any messages that elicit an inner knowing or response and empowers you to create the wholly beneficial life you desire.

The souls each had their own way of speaking and expressing their messages of love and evolution, and I want you to get the full sense of the experience, to "sit with us," since these messages were, in fact, meant for you. The following sessions are to help guide you in this life, understand your purpose here and now and after this life, and know that you are never alone in your pursuit for meaning, purpose, and answers. All answers are available to you in companionship with God, our Divine Guiding Presence, and the loving souls for which you share this evolutionary experience.

Learning happens at the level of your soul, not simply at the level of thought, although thought is always a part of the totality of your learning and existence. As you read each session, relax your analytical mind and simply allow the words to spark any innate knowing and rest on that, and then go about your daily tasks. Answers and guidance are often revealed when you least expect and you may start to notice how your life begins to flow with new energy simply by the awareness of the Divine messages and teachings within these sessions.

In all transparency, upon releasing these messages from Spirit and sharing my parent's deeply personal experiences, as well as fully accepting my own purpose of spreading the message of God's love and the divine gifts we are each forged with upon entering this life, I became a bit apprehensive. Not because I had any question of my purpose or the truth or validity of the events or the words spoken, but because I knew that such subjects go far beyond what our daily lives allow us to experience on Earth, thus it requires additional faith and an acknowledgment of our own divinity.

I started writing for and organizing the sessions for this book after looking deeply into my own life experiences, purpose, truths, lessons, challenges and successes, and recognizing my shift to living a more conscious life—acknowledging it from both a karma perspective and that of living in constant companionship with God. I have never so outwardly shared my beliefs, personal experiences and divine experiences so publicly, yet here I am. And I am here because of you because I am like you; we are both a part of a love so incredible and so beyond words. No matter where either of us is in our evolution, we are equal in the eyes of God and worthy of all things good.

It is through these sessions that I understand the gift of this life and the divine reasons for the heartbreak and challenges I personally have experienced. Nothing is promised in this life except the justice within one's heart, which you will read more about in the sessions that follow. My hope is that you too will see your life as a gift and one in which you are divinely guided.

I am reminded through these sessions that there are always loving souls guiding and supporting every aspect of our existence and evolution. They have helped us choose our method and time of entry, the circumstance of our birth, the family in which we are born into, and the set of challenges that await us, for the sole purpose of learning and maturing deeper into the divine energy of God.

Several times as I explored and found my own personal meaning in the following sessions, I felt the collective love of Spirit, of God, and of Jesus who, as you will read, all shared deeply profound messages. Reading these words, I felt that they knew me. And they know you. They know about the contrast that this Earth reality, your life, presents. They know of your willingness and decision to come into this life and your purpose for doing so. They are your support, your companion and your collaborator.

If you have ever felt that sense of overwhelming love within your heart, even if it is just a fleeting moment, you have touched upon this love of which I speak. It is the seed of all that you are created to be. You are empowered to create anything you choose to envision for your life, here, now and forevermore.

CORE TEACHINGS

Before you begin reading these nightly sessions with Spirit, I want to share some thoughts and insights that may help you navigate the teachings within the sessions. You may find many of these teachings simple to understand, accept and grasp, and others more challenging to fully comprehend the meaning behind them. Whatever the case, I invite you to relax on the words and allow whatever meaning to reveal itself.

You will find various messages repeated throughout the book. I have taken these messages and created nine core teachings to highlight their importance in your life here and now. So, with that said, before you read the following sessions, let's explore the main core teachings. By doing so, you will get a sense of how these teachings immediately apply to your life and your soul's healing and maturation into wholeness.

CORE TEACHING ONE
The Gift of Love, Thought, and Free Will

The first core teaching relates to what we are forged with upon coming into this life. Part of the purpose of all souls is to understand the three supreme truths of love, thought, and free will. (See Core Teachings Two through Five for details on each of these three truths.) Each is its own separate truth to understand, yet they can't function or be of benefit without the other.

"Behind all endeavor and understanding lies the truth
of love, thought, and free will."
—WISE ONE, TUESDAY, OCTOBER 19, 1982, SESSION 250

What is learned from Spirit is that thought creates, free will expresses, and love is the foundation that functions and guides. Our soul evolves to understand what it inherently knows upon its creation. What it knows is that the infinite supreme thought that creates soul, and all of existence, is the thought of "love given," a love without condition. And through love given, free will manifests itself through expression, and only when expressed through the energy of love given, can love grow and a better, fuller life be lived.

It is only through experience that you, as soul, can fully understand the divine love inherent within you. You must live enough experiences (reincarnations) to come to this truth.

CORE TEACHING TWO
Love is the Seed of All and All Have Love Inherent Within Them

Love is more than a warm fuzzy feeling in your heart or a feeling of passion or deep affection for another, which is often confined by condition. Love does something. It is who you are. A heart that is moved by love cannot sit idly by while another suffers. It is a light and an energy, and this energy is what gives you life and guides your growth and evolution. Love exists in every moment of every day, even in the midst of devastation or destruction.

Love is also a feeling of expansion. Imagine watching an inspirational video or story, or even just experiencing your child lovingly engaging with you, and without any effort on your part, tears well in your eyes, because for a moment, you realize once again the beauty of life; it is a reminder that just as you are created with love, it is inherent in your Being and you are born to love. This is the "reality" of love in this Earthly life. It is pure. It is unconditional.

"Love is all that and more for it exists and guides and is the infinite reality that none can escape and that all shall evolve to. For love forgives all, seeks all, accepts all. And love is just. And all that understand love, experience just endeavors. . . . Love the justice in your heart, mind, and soul, for that is what you shall have."
—WISE ONE, NOTEBOOK #35 PAGE 15

As the title implies, *Love is the Seed,* is an exploration into the very foundation of creation, all creation, with love being the seed of all creation. This concept, and understanding of the depths of love, is so far beyond what the human mind can even fathom or process and interpret through mere thinking. Love is the seed of all creation—ALL creation, right down to every atom and molecule. If you could see the amount of love within every atom and molecule, you would be overwhelmed.

These sessions with Spirit are a reminder that God is love and God created you, and all souls, out of the light of pure love. Within you, then, is God and love is inherent in your very being. The messages within these sessions are a reminder of this love and are meant to help you understand the true empowerment of love within you.

Just as a tree grows from a seed, sprouts a sapling, grows a sturdy base and stems branches and leaves, giving breath to the world around it, so do you—for you are, at your seed, love. Love is the seed of all creation, of all Being, of All.

"I write of love and am still not able to describe the truth of love, for no words can fully express the truth of love but the word 'love' itself."
—EDGAR CAYCE, MONDAY, DECEMBER 28, 1981, NOTEBOOK #26 PAGE 8

CORE TEACHING THREE
A Love Given is a Love Received, is a Just Solution for Life

How can knowing the truth of love change your life, right here and now? It is summed up in two sentences, "A love given is a love received. That is a just solution for life." This is referred to many times within the sessions. So, what does it mean?

All is given out of love. What you can understand from this is the just nature of karma; be it good karma or bad karma, it is just. It explains the reason for a lifetime after lifetime of conditioning existence, ultimately learning the true nature of love and learning ways in which you can embody this love; love being the infinite divine state of dynamic love, mercy, grace, compassionate wisdom, and empowerments.

At this very moment in your evolution, it is through love that you are your natural self. "Love given" is the law of God and the truth of creation. "Love given" grows and returns. You, as the personality living out this life, will receive what you give. If you choose to give respect, you will receive respect. If you choose to give fear, you will receive fear. If you choose to give love, you will receive love. For what is given justly from the heart, mind, and soul is returned, always. When you are giving, you are expressing the highest eternal thought.

The justice that is spoken of can be explained as understanding that in Divine mercy, as a state of being, there is "justness" in that it brings some to ultimate redemption and others for more karmic learning. There is always justice and this justice is always of love.

For perspective, if you are tied up in the vibrations of anger or jealousy, being in the realm of "love held closely," you go to a vibrational plane of anger and jealousy and remnants of those vibrations are carried throughout the evolution of your soul until you are awakened to the truth of love.

In a "love given" state, a heightened-awareness energy grows within you, and the things around you begin to change. You have heard the saying, "change your thoughts, change your life." Much the same, when love is being consciously lived and expressed through you, your vibration heightens, attracting more of the same. A love given is a love received. This is the justice of love. This shift, however small, changes the way you see the world and yourself. You begin to see things in a new way.

> *"The wisest understand that what is created from the heart,*
> *the honest integrity from within given freely to all,*
> *receives back the same multiplied many times."*
> —WISE GUIDE, SATURDAY, JUNE 12, 1982, SESSION 185

CORE TEACHING FOUR
"Thought" Lives on and Impacts Your Life Here and Now, and Beyond This Life

Why must you understand "thought" in the evolution of your soul and in this shared reality that is your life on Earth? Because thought is truly powerful. It can either empower you or hold you back from the learning, growing and fulfilling of what you must do in this karmic life for the evolution of your soul and for the pure enjoyment of living in this present moment. Thought will create anything that you wish. Thought creates each experience and in fact makes each experience what it is. Like-thoughts attract. Positive loving thoughts grow, and a love given grows and returns. Conversely, negative thoughts attract negative thoughts and negative energy.

You as "Knower Soul," being forever connected to divine love and wisdom, are currently in this shared reality on Earth, expressing through your human body and personality for a dual purpose—divine maturation and to fully enjoy living a purposeful, vibrant and fully "alive" life in human form. Thought relates to this dual purpose yet is its own entity and carries an energy that stays with you, even at a soul level, after this life.

So what thoughts are you holding onto that are suffocating the true, loving nature of your soul, slowing your growth and making this life more challenging? It is thought that has gotten you exactly where you are in evolution. Each personality on Earth is at the particular part of life that they are because of their past thoughts on Earth and because of their soul's justice.

Thoughts carry a vibration all their own and they seek out like-thoughts that carry the same vibration. So, if you are carrying negative thoughts, there will always be like-thoughts and like-vibration returned back to you. Thoughts are tied with fear and when you get stuck in your thoughts, there is no advancement or improvement in happiness; there is just a build-up of fear and it feeds off itself and others of the same vibration.

To hang onto a thought is to remain in a particular energy field for as long as the thought is hung onto. So, when you hang onto a negative thought, you will stay in this low-level energy field until that thought is let go. Like with all creations, thoughts themselves become multidimensional within their own vibrational level and live on within there.

When the soul is focused within any reality, it is focused by the method of "thought creation" and there is an infinite law of God and truth that says, "that which is created through thought lives forever as a free will creation." Ask yourself what you want this creation to be, in this life and then beyond this one life. You live many lives reincarnating for the purpose of learning and spiritually maturing in what one can call, the cocoon of life. You are constantly growing, maturing and transforming into something sincerely beautiful.

It is in relaxation or meditation into the stillness of a moment, a centering field of aware knowing, that you can bring yourself into a field that is beyond thinking and beyond the emotions caused by the thinking. It is on the other side of this still guiding presence that answers, enlightenments, and revelations are revealed, not through thought.

For example, when you write a poem or create in any form, it begins with a thought or idea. When you begin to create, you get into a zone or flow and the creation seems to create itself, effortlessly. Thought seems to no longer be present, for you are in the flow of creation and in fact creating out of the love for creating.

The sooner you can harness the power of your thoughts in a way that they become of complete service to you, as Soul, the better.

CORE TEACHING FIVE
Free Will Transformed into Wholly Beneficial Conscious Decisions

In the spiritual sense, free will is a truth each soul is forged with upon coming into this life in form. Free will is an enormous gift. You have the power to create any reality and make any moment what you desire. And conversely, you have the free will to make choices that are not of your highest benefit. The empowerment that comes from this gift of free will is when you begin to understand that this free will is really an opportunity for you to make wholly beneficial conscious decisions based on the foundation, or the seed, of love.

This is a core teaching that can truly transform your life, your decisions, your way of thinking and the actions that you take because when you understand this perspective of free will as wholly beneficial conscious decisions, you enter a giving space of allowing divinity's wholly beneficial enlightened energy field to live through you.

The benefits of making wholly beneficial conscious decisions directly affect your life here and now, your soul's maturation and all others involved and impacted. "Wholly beneficial conscious decisions" lovingly combines the highest aspects of who you are and your divine journey, with your personal life in form on this Earth experience. In making wholly beneficial conscious decisions, rather than just free will choice, it is also a vow that you will do no harm unto yourself or others.

Inevitably there may be times that you feel trapped in a circumstance, creating doubt that you have free will to choose your direction or outcome. Whether imprisoned physically or imprisoned within the mind or imprisoned within the structure of your society, no matter the circumstance, you always have free will to create and free will to live in alignment with God's laws. Each reincarnation gives your soul—being made up of many self-evolving free will personalities—the opportunity to create your life based on wholly beneficial conscious decisions in alignment with the love from which you are created.

> *"For through free will, one travels many paths in pursuit of truth.*
> *When those about you are not in agreement with what you know,*
> *then look within and ask for guidance, it is there."*
> —Jesus, January 31, 1982, Session 105 Page 3

CORE TEACHING SIX
All Are Created Equally in the Eyes of God

You have a story—many stories, in fact, over lifetimes. And each lifetime, a self-evolving personality as a part of your soul. Within this particular lifetime, you are born into a different set of circumstances, physical body, environment, and upbringing. Regardless of appearance, color, race, dialect, level of intelligence, and social status, whether described as a "good person" or a "bad person," who speaks "too soft" or "too harsh," "too loud" or "too quiet," whatever the belief or reality may be, you, and each, are created equally in the eyes of God.

You may find it difficult to see God in others and wonder how God has created all equally and all out of love, when there are those out there who create devastation, spread hate, and harm others. How can they possibly be created equally and out of the same energy of divine love that you were created? With the layers upon layers of history, beliefs, man-made structures, laws and a collective unconsciousness that exists, it can be especially difficult. It can be easy to overlook the love that exists each day and in each person. Yet love will, nonetheless, always reveal itself. It can be as simple as a small gesture of kindness or selflessness—of giving without the expectation of receiving anything in return.

This core teaching that all are created equally in the eyes of God, is important to understand because it speaks to the divine justice of this life. Each day, you share your space with millions of souls each on their own journey of self-discovery and karmic learning, and each at their own level of knowing, within the evolution of the soul. This means that inevitably your life is full of contrast—good things, bad things, good people and bad people. So, all are created equally in the eyes of God because all—no matter "good" or "bad"— are created with love at the seed and each living out their justice. And this justice is always given out of divine love.

> *"All are created equally in the eyes of God and God loves all equally.*
> *God has willed that none shall perish who do not want to perish,*
> *and that created out of love given, which is All, shall never perish,*
> *for it is not in their infinite desire for selfhood."*
> —WISE ONE, NOTEBOOK #29 PAGE 17

CORE TEACHING SEVEN
Error is the Path to Growth

> *"Love is the knowledge that error is human. Love is the*
> *understanding that error in the pursuit of love is just and*
> *the love in the pursuit of error is not just."*
> —JESUS, NOTEBOOK #22 PAGE 3

This Earth experience is a karmic learning experience. There is always a purpose for entering and re-entering life after life in form. This purpose is usually not a singular purpose, but rather a group of purposes consisting of a soul purpose, a debt purpose (resolving karma), and a loving and contributing purpose.

Earth is one of many schoolhouses for the soul to learn. Challenge is inevitable. Error is inevitable. And, fortunately, growth is inevitable.

This error can account for the injustices in the world. There will always be a contrast, wrong-doings, and a collective unconscious at work. It is inevitable for the sake of learning. Fortunately, too, there will always be love and a collective higher consciousness and awareness, and humans living a higher purpose to counter-balance the negative.

You, as Soul, have inherent within you the God-given talent and free will to create. You can create harmony, or you can create havoc. Each has their own justice. What you cannot be given is understanding, because understanding comes about by not just observing and trying to comprehend and analyze with the mind, but from doing. And in doing, you must make mistakes, for unless you know the contrast, you cannot find your truth. So, dramas are created and lived for the sake of learning. Unfortunately, in this Earth experience, these dramas can be devastating, heart-breaking and confusing, yet all are errors for the sake of learning.

> *"It is better to pursue an error than to sit and stagnate,*
> *for there is no growth and no understanding."*
> —WISE GUIDE, NOTEBOOK #35 PAGE 15

CORE TEACHING EIGHT
Death of the Body is a New Opportunity for Your Soul to Learn

What you will learn from the sessions with Spirit is that there is more than just this Earth experience. And once you leave this life, your soul has the opportunity to rest, contemplate and reflect. In the afterlife, you learn in a similar way as in your Earth experiences, but without the same type of stress you feel here. There is a greater understanding that love is truth and that life is infinite. You go through learning experiences and they are of your own choosing and understanding. It is possible, you will read in the sessions that follow, to create psychodramas in the spirit world for further development of your soul, much like this Earth experience can be thought of as a psychodrama of karma through which you learn.

> *"Whether here or in another alternative experience*
> *the process is learning, understanding, battling, for that*
> *infinite wisdom that manifests the soul's true nature, and*
> *in all souls that nature, that thought, is Love."*
> —Wise One, Friday, November 27, 1981, 10 p.m. Session 59

CORE TEACHING NINE
You Don't Have to "Do It" Alone

The good news is that you don't have to personally mature yourself. There is a Ninety-Nine Percent Element of Divinity at work on your behalf. What this means is that as you tend to your daily tasks at hand and you pursue from a loving heart, for every step that you take toward doing and learning, Divinity—God—is taking ninety-nine steps for your benefit.

So, tend to what you desire and need to and know that in the energy of true enlightening love, grace and mercy for which you are a part and where you ultimately become harmoniously united with, in order, balance and in companionship to wholeness, is at work.

Lastly, putting aside all complexities and your eager efforts to fully understand your life here, now and beyond this life, what is most important now, in this moment and as you go about this Earthly experience, is simply to relax, to love and to appreciate. You are in God's hands here, now and forevermore.

PROLOGUE

Sitting next to him on the sofa after putting their three young children to bed—ages six, almost three, and one—she was unsure of what to expect. My father, Mike, sat quietly in meditation. My mother, Kathleen, patiently waited. Suddenly his head flew back, mouth gaped open taking in a gasp and his entire body began to shake. Moments later, he was quiet, eyes closed, and body relaxed.

That was when the souls came through, and the sessions began.

It would be the first of many souls channeling through my father, in what would be their eleventh year of marriage. My mother would sit to his left every night, for two years, 1981 and 1982, and take dictation. She filled notebooks as fast as she could, writing every word that was spoken. The souls came forth with the intention of writing two books—the first of which you are holding in your hands.

Despite the way in which my parents experienced divine presence, I imagine that they are much like you. Their lives have been comprised of challenges and triumphs, anger and forgiveness, attachment and detachment, love and loss, feelings of being lost and knowing that they are never really lost, and they teetered at times between questioning everything and innately knowing their connection to God.

Your individual path through life and your spiritual journey are unique and although rough at times, can take you to places you have never imagined. This book is a testament to a part of my parent's journey and a promise kept that the messages contained herein would make it into the hands of those who need it most, for the benefit of mankind. This part of their journey together was enlightening and exhilarating at times and confusing and challenging at other times, as they did their individual best to maintain a "normal" family life.

My mother, the kindest, hardest working and most selfless woman—a woman who would take our spare blankets from home to cover homeless people who were sleeping on the streets at night after getting off from her second job. My father, a man who came into this life knowing that he is here for a higher purpose, partly fulfilled when he met and had children with my mother, and partly fulfilled through his decades-long comprehensive spiritual journey.

Just before that first evening, my mother recalls my father telling her of a time he was in his office alone sitting in silence, about to begin his typical 20-minute meditation before going home. Prior to his meditation on this particular afternoon, he said a prayer. In this prayer, he asked, if it be God's will, to be shown his past lives and his soul's purpose. And with that prayer, in meditation, he was taken on what felt like an inner rollercoaster ride going backward. At each stop, there was a hologram that represented him in a past life—male or female—and a sense of the experience of that life.

He did this for three weeks, but he was still unclear of his soul's purpose for continued reincarnation in form, so he made a different request for clarification. Upon this request, he was taken through various divine experiences and countless existences on inner planes in meditation, at first with Divine Presence and an unnamed guide, and then alone. Within this experience, he was guided into a pure, aware, clear, blissful white light. Expanding out were rays and light realms beyond measure, and he could see and feel light beings within those realms. There was an awareness of the presence of God and an inner knowing of a greater purpose. My father had been absorbed into the light of pure love, confirming for him that the base of all is love—the light of God. He was then asked to pick up a pen and write. He told my mother that he knew he wasn't doing the writing, so he continued, and the pen continued to move.

Unbeknownst to us, my father was terrified when this all began to happen—partly because of his willingness to open himself to whatever was awaiting him (be it to experience "heaven" or "hell"), and partly because he knew that things were going to change, and he was concerned with what would happen to his family. He had prayed for this family that he had been gifted with, and now, he was going to fully commit to this journey—a journey that goes well beyond what is documented in this book.

What my mother witnessed during the two years of channeled sessions confused and silenced her. Between this extraordinary event—for which she felt deeply grateful to the loving souls—and my father's journey trying to now balance a "spiritual" and "Earthly" life, she lost a bit of herself, and it would take years to start regaining the normalcy that she once had.

One day my father no longer needed my mother to take dictation of the sessions. He was fully immersed into his journey and was able to accomplish what he needed on his own—soul travel, gain answers and write. Eventually, my parents both agreed that it would be best to part ways, which I believe in part gave them both a renewed sense of excitement, the freedom to live their lives in the ways that made them feel most fulfilled, and experience in their own unique way the love with which they were created.

As expressed within the following pages, *"Love is a feeling that your body and mind is exhilarated. It is a feeling of good. It is a feeling of great. It is a feeling of grandeur. Love is understanding that God is All, and All is God. Love is the method by which you shall find the nature of the true creative process. Love given without expectations. Love received without expectations. Love is a way of obtaining wisdom. Love is a way of all."*

The text contained herein is information from various loving souls, each excited to share their messages of love, consciousness, death and reincarnation, God's laws and creation, and it contains answers to questions that you may be asking yourself when in search of your own enlightenment and sense of purpose here on Earth and beyond.

These intimate conversations with various guides, mystics, religious leaders, and other loving souls offer the opportunity to reconnect to the love of God, a passage to discover your own personal purpose and reinforce your inner knowing that kindness, love, and better understanding can heal your life.

Rather than reading this book through from cover to cover, it would be far more beneficial to read one session at a time wherever you choose to begin, pausing at, and perhaps rereading whatever passages that elicit an inner knowing or response.

Each session was written exactly word for word as the souls spoke through my father. Some sessions may include various thoughts and topics, and from different souls coming forth. Some passages may not initially make sense. All of the sessions are presented in the souls' free-flowing thought. Sometimes my father would have an inner dialog with a soul. If a sentence seems to stop, it is because "thought" was being used to communicate. When you see "Date Unknown," or no date or notebook number is mentioned, it is because there was no documented date for the session or the session was separate from a specific notebook.

Before each session began, the souls coming through would often introduce themselves and each spoke with love, excitement, curiosity, kindness, and purpose.

Mike Rice is one of the first souls who spoke. He told my mother and father that he used to work with my great-grandmother in San Francisco. Edgar Cayce, an American clairvoyant, spoke many times for the purpose of giving wise words to help write this book. The personality of Seth (I and II) also visited many times. Dorothy Jane Roberts was an American author, poet, self-proclaimed psychic, and spirit medium, who claimed to channel energy who called himself "Seth," a personality no longer focused in physical reality.

With everything that is happening in the world, you may be yearning for solace, yearning for meaning, yearning for answers, yearning to restore your hope and faith, and yearning to reconnect with who you are: a loving creation and extension of God. As the dialogs that follow make clear: love is the seed.

I now invite you to imagine yourself sitting with my mother and father during these nightly sessions and feel how the words resonate with the core of your Being. The intention of the souls coming forth was to share these messages for you.

CHAPTER 1

LOVE

Love is an official duty of all mankind.
Love is the link—the common thread
that connects all life.

Love is understanding that each element is contributing to
each element and that all are created equally in God's eyes.
That God is in each and each is a part of God.

CHAPTER 1

LOVE

The souls wanted the first chapter to be called Love. They speak of the beginning of all creation and of how love is the seed of all creation—the common element that binds us all. Each soul is created with the primary intention of love, and with that comes thought and free will. Through this forged free will and natural pursuit of service through love, man and all soul forms choose their path or their role. They emphasize what it means to understand that all are created equally in God's eyes.

All have love, and through love, you are given the innate knowing of who you are and the confidence to see that love is the common measure that is in others, and the contributing element that connects us with God. They remind us that we are all connected and when you think "love" from the depth of your being, it has a soothing effect on your mind. And because the mind is directly linked to the body and the seven centers of the body, it can bring harmony from within and the capacity to harmonize and connect more deeply with others.

So, come sit with us.
These messages are meant for you.

(DICTATION BEGINS)

❀ IN THE BEGINNING

Date Unknown
This is a Wise One speaking.

In the beginning, there was God, the creative force that has created all that you know and all that you do not yet know. Out of love, God cast forth many souls. The soul goes back to the beginning, to God, from whence it came. The soul has recorded all its pain and glory, and the glory is in the Lord. The Lord loves all and receives the soul with love.

God is with all men. Man will one day be with God. God does not forsake any man but wishes man would not forsake God. God is love, light, and truth.

God is All. All is God. Each is God. God is Each. Within each and all does God dwell. God asks only that you ask for the voice of God to be heard. Ask and the voice of God will begin from within, you will hear and dream messages.

Interpret not those messages as mankind interprets and defines. Love for the love behind and within the message. Simply think and pray what you wish God to be. There will be the measure of God that will have answered.

God is love, truth, thought, and will.

God is in you.

The answer is in you.

The only part of you found in others and that which binds you to others is love. All have love. Through love, all can find confidence in themselves and find that measure of themselves that exists in others.

❀ HOW ONE UNDERSTANDS LOVE

Notebook #35, Page 15, Monday, February 1, 1982, Session 106
This is your Wise Guide.

God has created all in God's image and God's image is love. How then does one understand love? One understands love through the soul's vision. The soul evolves through infinite expression of freely given experience. Humans and all on Earth and throughout Earth's solar system are reflections and freely evolving souls within the infinity of all.

God has created all equally through God's infinite thought of love and God has forged all with free will. The soul newly created knows this but cannot understand this, for understanding comes through that forged free will that endows each soul the freedom to create, as of course, God does. For is that not God's image to create?

God has created all equally. The equalness lies in the creation of the soul. The soul is thought, love, and free will forever.

The essence is the reality of experience, the reality of experience relates to the purpose. Purpose is essence. Essence is the purpose.

Experience is the working out of evolutionary understanding. The soul endowed with God's image of God's thought, love, and free will, creates a just experience.

Love is evolving to understand that the justice in the soul's heart, mind, and vision is that which the soul shall have.

Cycles within cycles. Love within love. Justice within justice. Order within order. Thought within thought. Free will within free will. Ever turning, ever-evolving, ebbing and flowing into the waters of soul's evolution. All that is, is truth. Truth is all that is. God is truth. Truth is God.

The soul, "new soul" evolves through orders, cycles, justice, free will, thought and love, always love.

The old soul has evolved through all of the aforementioned and yet may evolve again if said soul has not more than knowledge, and what is more than knowledge, is understanding.

Earth's solar system is one of many and one like all others is an expression of experience. God's solar system is truth, and truth is love, free will, and thought, none of these exist without the other.

The Earth's solar system is a mere reflection of truth and all upon Earth are reflections of operational truth. Souls on Earth are of a finding nature. There are some experiences of a practicing nature and some of a guiding nature and some of a creating nature.

All systems reflect truth. However, a soul must find and understand truth before functioning within other systems. There are other systems of a different vibratory level that are of a finding nature, also.

The paths to God are many and traveled many times over by some souls. Structures change and adapt as evolutionary experiences change and adapt. There are teachers within all systems.

POWER OF PATIENCE *(Same Session)*

This is a Wise One.

Patience is love. Patience is understanding. Patience is accepting that all things in the evolution of the soul are infinite existence of God. Patience is giving and receiving with love, living and believing in love. Patience, for all return to God. Remember that you are destined to return to God. That you should live your life accordingly.

Love is a remarkable thought for mankind. Love is a patient thought for mankind. Love is understanding that all man, inspire to do good. All are equal under God's eyes.

Love is an understanding that all men are born to choose their destinies. Love is an understanding that all men are forced to live in a world that is forged with free will.

Love is the good will that man does and thinks and is. Love is the good will that man creates and is. Love is the good will that man has in his heart and shares with mankind. Love is good. That man has love in his heart and shares it with mankind is good.

Love is the method by which you shall find the nature of the true creative process. Love given without expectations. Love received without expectations. Love is understanding that all is God and God is all. That all were created equally in the eyes of God. Love is a feeling that your body and mind is exhilarated. It is a feeling of good. It is a feeling of great. It is a feeling of grandeur. Love is the method of attaining wisdom. Love is a way of all.

A love given is a love received. A forged free will is love's creative thought. Honor the free will of each.

Love's being is the core of evolutionary existence. Love's being is a freely given thought. Love's being is understanding that free will is forged upon each element and is God's love. Love is be-ing—being is love. All is God and God is love.

✿ SOUL'S NATURE *(Same Session)*

The need for each element, each personality, is love. Love can be described as needing purpose. Purpose will manifest drive, desire, hope, visualization, and a more fulfilled Earth experience. Purpose should be shared to be reinforced. Needs are fulfilled through visualization. Needs can be fulfilled through fear if that is the choice.

For the most fulfilled life that brings the greatest amount of eternal peace, face fears and share your vision with all about you.

Love, the supreme thought and only truth and reality, is freely given and endowed. All are created equally in the eyes of God.

To understand the soul's nature, the soul evolves through just experience in an ordered evolutionary process. And ordered evolutionary process endows each soul with multidimensional expression over time, space, and essence, the essence, being purpose.

✿ ESSENCE AND SOUL'S EXPRESSION *(Same Session)*

The essence is the reality of experience. The reality of experience relates to the purpose. Purpose is the essence. Essence is the purpose.

Mankind, animal-kind, plant-kind, earth-kind, and star-kind represent some of the infinite orders of the soul's expression. The soul's expression is justly ordered and justly experienced. Experience is the working out of evolutionary understanding.

The soul endowed with God's image, of God's thought, love and free will, creates a just experience.

The greatest wisdom is also the greatest truth existing forever, as God exists forever over time, space, and purpose.

The greatest truth is love, the supreme thought that is endowed with the freedom to evolve to understanding and eternal happiness.

All is God. God is All. Love is All. All is Love.

✾ LOVE AND TRUTH *(Same Session)*

Truth is within each soul, each thought, each being, each order, each manifestation, each reality, each creation, no matter what.

Truth operates upon the laws of thought, love, and free will. All actions are because of and in response to thought, love and free will. Each system of reality no matter when focused, exhibits a reaction to this truth. On Earth, with the system or order of the human being, there exist many man-made structures, concepts, beliefs, governments, societies, individuals, theories, and all exhibit and function within truth, love, free will and thought.

Love is the highest 'thought' and exists in all.

Within all systems, all elements, every fiber of beingness, every reality, love transcends and permeates all.

Love is all that and more, for it exists and guides, and is the infinite reality that none can escape and that all shall evolve to. For love forgives all, seeks all, accepts all. And love is just. And all that understand love, experience just endeavors.

✾ LOVE IN JUSTICE *(Same Session)*

The justice that we speak of is the justice that each and all shall determine for themselves by thought and experience. And yet the beauty of justice is that it is love. Love the justice in your heart, mind, and soul, for that is what you shall have.

Love is the Supreme Being, All That Is, All. Love is the truth that is part of all. Love is the reality of creation. Love is the understanding that all are created equally in the eyes of God. Love is the reality of the justice that is in the soul shall be had. Love is the patience of understanding that the truth to creation is the thought of love and that the justice is in love and that the resolve will seek out the truth.

✾ LOVE, SERVICE, AND JUSTICE

Notebook #22, Page 9

This is a Wise One. We will discuss love and service and justice.

All were born out of love (and) forged with free will. All are in service for the understanding of love and all that is and all that will be and has been. Through this forged free will in pursuit of this service of love, man and all soul forms choose a path and a role.

When souls are and were and will be first created, they understand and feel the warmth of love. But through love and free will all souls have a natural desire to create and a natural desire to experience that which is created in some way or another.

Now there really are no levels but there are degrees of understanding that come about through experience.

What the soul determines (pursues) and learns by choice is the guiding influence. Now the portion of the soul that represents the personality or personalities is evolving too and has set goals or purposes for entering this earth's experience. These are entered into, what one might call, "scientifically," for the order can be learned and there are properties to the physical manifestation of the soul that do indeed relate to mass and energy. Those properties have not yet been learned.

In the order of Earth's experience, one determines the area of interest that one will follow.

Notebook #23, Page 12
This is a Wise One.

The nature of love is such that when one thinks Love from the depth of their being, it has a soothing effect on one's mind, and the mind is directly linked to the body and the seven centers of the body are as close to harmony as the individual soul level indicates.

Notebook #23, Page 15
This is a Wise One.

Love is the understanding that one and all are God and God is one and all.

I Am that I Am.
I Am the Beginning.
I Am the Ending.
I Am Never Ending.
I Am That I Am.
In the beginning, there is no beginning, but there was I Am.

There was a thought of love.

There was a soul of love.

There were many souls of love on many firmaments.

There are infinite souls that are a part of the I Am and each is forged with love and each is forged with creating and each is forged with free will. That love that each and all consciousness possess is the seed of being. The love that all possess is the seed of creation.

The justice that each possess is the love of God that through forged free will all will individually and collectively create their destiny and path to the truth. The truth is that love is the seed of all creation, of all being, of all.

I Am that I Am. When one understands the nature of love then one becomes a part of, I Am That I Am.

To become one with I Am that I Am is not to self-annihilate but to understand. To become one with I Am That I Am is to find one's own true individual and collective nature.

I Am That I Am has the love for all at the seed of I Am That I Am. I Am That I Am is true consciousness. Love. Bless you and all. Bless your family and all.

🏵 LEVELS CREATED FOR THE SOUL *(Same Session)*

The firmament is all that all think. The God is the highest level of all. And Each.

There are levels that are created for the soul to understand that one individual soul is gaining. There are seven Earth levels, they are:

1. Earth
2. Casual
3. Astral
4. Heaven
5. Revelation
6. Acceptance
7. Understanding mental, mind, consciousness, love.

That all can be created through love and love is thought and gives greater energy and being, than any other thought, is the truest understanding of all that is.

✿ LOVE AS SUPREME THOUGHT: EDGAR CAYCE

Monday, December 28, 1981, Notebook #26, Page 8
This is Edgar Cayce.

I have been a speaker of God for eons of time. I write of love and am still not able to describe the truth of love, for no words can fully express the truth of love, but the word "love" itself. For love is the supreme thought by which all are created.

Love's wisdom is the patient resolve to understand that which one cannot change, one should accept, that which one cannot accept, one should change. Through the thought of love, God created all equally loving. To understand equality is to understand love in its purest form. To understand love in its purest form is to live in the truth that all are created equally in the eyes of God.

✿ SOUL AND LOVE

Notebook #31, Page 10
This is a Wise One.

The soul gives out of love. The soul receives out of love. The soul exists out of love given. The soul is infinite out of given and received love. The soul of self creates for the self. The soul that creates for the self has nothing to receive but self-love. Love for the self turns to fear and nonunderstanding, and there are certain inherent reactions that come about because of this.

One who loves for the self will try and steal and demand from others what it is unable to give itself. One who loves to give will not have to steal, for what is received is freely returned manifold.

If you give to many, you receive from many. If you give to few, you receive from few. If you give to one, you receive from one. If you hold love to the self, there it stays. If a tree held all its fruit, the fruit would rot, if the fruit given from the tree is not consumed it rots. A tree gives freely its fruit.

The fruit is freely consumed. The consumed waters the tree, the tree grows more fruit. Who will water the tree? Who will hold its fruit? What would become of the tree that held its fruit? Now the tree is you, and the fruit is love. What pray tell is becoming of you?

THE SELF-DEFEATING ASPECT OF LOVE

Sunday, January 10, 1982, Session 88

This is your Wise Guide.

All that personalities experience in some manner are reflections of love. All is thought, the personality is thought, the personality is a thought of love, just as all elements are thoughts of love. The personality experiences reflections of love, perceptions of love. When the personality is seeking self-love then the personality is working against the thought of love. When the personality is in the pursuit of self-love, love taken not given, love expecting, then the personality is pursuing a self-defeating aspect of love.

We will conclude there for this evening to gather thoughts on the subject of this negative aspect of love.

Do you have any general questions, specific questions, any questions about anything?

Kathleen: I have none.

Mike: Yes, I have a question and if you wish to answer it in a dream state then that's fine. My question relates to the inter-relationship between orders, how they assimilate and recreate. And that is all.

That is an infinitely wise question. That will be answered while dreaming.

Mike: And a quick question just to clarify my mind on the future—is the future being lived right now?

Yes

Mike: And yet the future can be changed?

Yes

Mike: As the past can be changed?

Yes

Mike: Can you more fully explain it?

That will be for another dream. For telling you will not give you understanding that will require reintroducing you to your systems.

(Note from the Author: In the decades following these sessions, my father continued to be taken through various planes, systems, lives, etc., through a series of divine-guided interventions, in meditation and in dream. He was called to experience the breadth of

all that Divine Guiding Presence had to share about the evolution of his soul, the countless experiences within divinity and Earthly "conditioned" life; this would ultimately all act as a testament for us all that we are much more than just this one Earthly life.)

Mike: *Thank you, I have no more questions.*

This is your Wise Guide. Are there any questions?

Mike: *No, I have none.*

Good Evening.

❀ WISDOM AND INFINITE LOVE

Monday, February 1, 1982, Session 106

This is your Wise Guide. We will now speak of wisdom and infinite love.

Wisdom is infinite understanding that love is the eternal truth. Truth is a given love and a given love is a received love. Wisdom is seeking through truth infinitely that which is eternal love. Eternal love is infinite seeking of a given love that is being. Thought is a love given freely and a freely given love is the thought of God. God is infinitely infallible, loving, giving. All is God and all seek understanding of God's infinitely infallible love. Love's "being" is the core of evolutionary existence.

Love's "being" is a freely given thought. Love's "being" is understanding that free will is forged upon each element and is God's love. Love is being—being is love. All is God and God is Love.

When a soul is created out of love there is free will forged upon that soul. That soul projects through thought those experiences in learning and understanding love. The soul who projects is at once closest and at once furthest from understanding love. To understand love, one soul or any element must give, experience and learn.

"Knowing" is taking someone or another soul's understanding and knowing it. Understanding love is reaching within and expressing without that love forged upon each, freely giving to all. It is better to pursue an error than to sit and stagnate for there is no growth and no understanding.

We will conclude for this evening. We say good evening. This is your Wise Guide. You may go now.

✿ MANKIND AND LOVE

Wednesday, February 17, 1982, Session 118
This is a Wise, Wise, Wise One. I Am That I Am.

For what does a man gain if he gains all the riches of the world and yet cannot find love.

Within each human being rests infinite love, love that bridges all faiths, religions, all songs, art, philosophies, politics. Mankind to a person expresses the many phases and facets of love; each human needs, desires, and hopes for love. Through creativity, whatever the endeavor, love is expressed giving of oneself to others.

All on Earth look to receive that gift that creativity gives and most look to return it and do indeed return that form of love-given many times.

When one sleeps, thinks, performs daily functions, exists, the eternal quest is love. Understand that love that exists within you and expresses that love. And you shall find a great deal more peace in your Earthly lives.

There are many opportunities to express love and seek and gain that understanding and all in one form or another are following the path of understanding love. Those on Earth that fellow humans determine as evil are part of God and within them there exists infinite love. Their yearning and expression will eventually, through eons of time, find truth.

Love is All. All is Love. All is God and God is All. When mankind as individuals begin to express that eternal love, begin to understand that all are created equal in God's eyes, begin to realize that the justice in your hearts you shall have, begin to accept each element and individual right of free will expression without judgment, where that free will expression does not infringe upon the rights of other individual elements free will expression, that each element of God has consciousness, then peace will exist.

That is all for this evening.

Friday, February 19, 1982, Session 119
This is a Wise One.

The nature of good and evil is one of love given and love held closely for there is no evil, just interpretations of love.

Now it has been said in the various writings that there are levels and steps, there are devils and gods, there are rights and wrongs, there are goods and evils, there are doing correctly with God and doing incorrectly with dark forces. There are many interpretations, many symbologies, many references to God through structure.

There are many paths to God. There is no right or wrong path. There is just learning. You *(meaning my father)* have just been reading a book in which they have talked about Mahatma the Christ and the Lords of Wisdom. In that book, they speak of communications with other beings including the Mahatma as the coming Christ. There will be many souls upon the world that are redirecting mankind's thinking. They are highly evolved souls and from a learning state, all symbology and structure does exist and is deemed necessary by learning beings.

The structures that are explained by learning beings are based upon learned information or transmitted information to various souls explaining symbolically steps towards God, so to beings on Earth, there is a structure developed. There are levels of understanding as souls go through experience. There are many souls alike, learning and understanding, who develop, require, request, pray, and meditate for a great leader.

Now it is said that mankind or the human is marked with color. When these structures are followed, there are indeed advancements made, understanding gained and love given. These structures needed by all form the basis or beliefs, attitudes, and actions.

Within each structured form, belief-patterned form, there exists that search—the search is for love, love given, and a fuller understanding of love given. There is not a single belief philosophy or person that will go to a heaven by following a "structure." There are wise understandings of love, thought, free will, justice, solace, projection, thought, and wisdoms that come through the application of love given. This love that exists and is–is the I Am, God that is within each.

When a soul finds its greater self, it finds its interpretation of love. When a soul finds understanding, it finds the multidimensionality of love and yet as multidimensional as love is, it is so simply, simply beautiful and there for each to express and give. It is that which knows, understands, and expresses no fear. Fear binds–love frees. Fear controls–love expresses. Fear holds–love gives. Fear is love seeking. Love is fear resolved.

Solace is inner reflection. Solace is peace. Solace is inner seeking. Solace is meditation. Solace is finding that peace within that is love.

Justice is that which the heart seeks and finds through expression. Justice is the reality of expression. Justice is the functioning of experience. Justice is karma, reincarnation, receiving, giving, understanding that—that which the soul gives is returned and that which the soul gives is an expression of love.

THE I AM OF LOVE *(Same Session)*

This is your Wise Guide.

I Am that I Am. I am love that heals and binds and gives. I bind all together for all are a part of I Am. All are an expression of I Am. All are love—love is I Am.

It is what defines God, defines evolution, defines you; seek love and you find I Am. Seek love and I Am finds you.

I Am that I Am. I am with you always. Wherever you go I am. Whatever traps you I am there. Whatever frees you I am there. I am with all. Accept or reject but I am that is truth and reality.

Mike is shaking, a lot of shaking.

I Am that I Am. I am with you tonight. I am the love that binds, secures and expresses, I am All.

We will now say good evening.

Mike is shaking a lot, his eyes are tightly shut, now he is asleep again.

This is Jesus. I will be guiding and helping spread the words of love. Finally again, mankind will be introduced the greatest truths, the greatest realities in its most beautiful, its simplest terms. I bless you *(Mike's arm is on my back.)* I bless you.

Live freely without fear and guilt, for love is a fearless and guiltless reality. When I said render unto Caesar what to Caesar, I was merely saying, render unto the physical world what is the physical world and let them have it for truth goes on.

Mike's eyes are shut, and his arms are out slowly and now down, and he is shaking. Mike is back. No, his eyes are tight again! Now he is shaking. Mike asked for ice water—shaking—WIDE mouth.

Now you may go.

Sunday, June 20, 1982, Session 191

This is a Wise One.

As Earth's history cycles and changes there are those who choose to speak and live the word. The word is love. All come to understand love. In one method or another love is meant to be lived, given, and received.

Cycles are repeated, the same stories told in similar but different dramas, and yet the word never changes, never falters, however, the stories are told.

Giving is the most revered and honored act and giving of oneself is love. Giving starts in nowness when one makes the decision to begin. There is thought, there is free will, and there is that quality of thought that is allowed to express freely and the quality is love in its highest form.

Each within has a time, and many times when there was a need to fill the heart, to fill the soul, to fill the mind, and that need is for love.

All, all, all, are touched by love.

We will be with you tomorrow and always. You may now go. Praying can be done with a simple thought for all. Praying can be a moment of caring, a moment of giving.

Saturday, July 31, 1982, Session 211

This is a Wise One.

When the soul focuses in a physical element of God, be it plant, animal, man, atom, recalling that all elements possess the attributes of truth.

The smallest molecules themselves possess thought, love, and free will. Perspective exists within each element of God, plants, animals, man, atom, molecules. Each element exhibits and lives and perceives from its own unique perspective.

When one comes into contact with other orders, one does not and cannot perceive from the perspective of that order. One can relate to their order. When one is evolving to a state of understanding whereby one recognizes that all elements in Gods eyes have equal validity, equal value, equal capacity to think within their order and perspective.

The absolute value that exists in all that transcends all is love. It is the link between all. However, perceptions change the value of absolute love. Evolutionary understanding changes the value of absolute love.

However, love is absolute. There is God perspective and there is a supreme God, a loving God, a creating God that has created all. All shall ascend to this God.

Therefore, one human reading these words should be aware that they are evolving and are not yet princes of God, co-creators with God, livers, procreators with God. They are a part of God and God is a part of them. God is not their mind. God is not the soul's mind. God is not their free will. God can be their absolute love and is an interpretation of their expressed love through justice.

When one is focused in an individual perspective one will be most effective in changing all about them in expressing any love that they desire to express and creating any creations they desire to create in living freely by first understanding themselves wherever they may be in a given experience or an evolutionary understanding. And when understanding that, go forth and do with pure intention of being true unto oneself.

This does not mean fulfilling ones needs selfishly unless that is a true perspective, but simply understanding the known-self to the individual, going forth and expressing it.

We will conclude for this evening. You may go and relax.

Notebook #32, Page 6
This is a Wise One.

We will now speak of God. The human species like all elements of God is forged with free will born out of love given. The supreme thought of God by which ALL elements of God exists and develop.

ALL elements of God experience through order and function through justice.

ALL elements of God are infinite.

ALL created elements of God exist forever as a part of God and as a free will evolving element of all that is.

All elements do not choose to find the God Head at the same time or in the same manner.

When a soul merges with all souls of what is referred to as the "God Head" they function out of love given for the benefit of all consciousness forever. All and each element that is a part of the, what is called, the "God Head" are ALWAYS with free will. They always create and experience. That which is created out of love given and freely given is just, good, and loving.

HOW TO GIVE LOVE

Unknown Date
This is a Wise One.

Each has love to give. Each wants to give love. Humanity sometimes forces fake interpretation defining what love is and is not. Give love from your heart. Receive love from your heart. Love's desire can take on many forms depending upon the interpretation. A desire for love is a desire for comfort, companionship, and the opportunity to give of oneself the love that is within them.

Give to all what you feel within. Accept love given to you. Love all in all the ways that you can. Love is respecting the free will right of all and each. Accepting their right to give and their right to receive and their right to deny.

Love is God. God is love. Love is God and God's law of truth. Truth is the thought that love is the highest expression of God and all.

All possess creative ability by which to freely create. Creation freely expressed is the greatest act of love.

Love is understanding that all evolve justly and infinitely to understanding that God is love, thought, and free will, not one without the other.

Quality is hard to define because it is self-measured. If one says that you are great and a great thinker or a great something, that is merely their perception. In truth, you are either peaceful and content within yourself or are not peaceful and content within yourself. Wherever you go you carry your true self within you. You are what you think and will always be so. But you are not alone and trapped in that mind or body, for God has created ALL in God's image. God is thought, freely given; for God is patient and understanding and realizes that what is given is returned manifold.

God is so loving; God freely gives each soul God-given rights and truths of creating. God understands that the knowing soul will understand that the highest quality thought is love. That the laws of love operate on the principles of, a love given is a love received, a love held closely is a love held closely.

That justice in your heart, mind, and soul, you will have. What one creates out of thought, one shall have. That justice is the consequence of our thought. How much more loving and just can God be, than to allow each to create their own unique destiny and to reap all the benefits of what each creates. God creates each soul and the soul is thought, externally measured and marked by energy and color.

Soul evolves and learns to be with those supreme souls and God and beings which operate freely through love. Souls create, and one of the creating experiences is Earth. Souls create in an ordered manner, focusing through orders and not finding their true soul-self until they have evolved to understand truth.

Love is, as I Am is. God is I Am that I Am, forevermore.

God is thought that created all beings out of love forevermore.

All is God. God is All. All is Love. Love is All.

One can seek and strive to understand the nature of God and creation and life and evolution in many ways through various experiences using various structures and symbologies. The ultimate understanding is LOVE, is GOD. God is the thought of love. Love and thought are truth, are God, and all. Those are the ultimate truths by which ALL function. Supreme being, supreme thought, supreme truth is Love, Love is God and God is All.

I love all. All loves me. All deserve my love and respect. I deserve All's love and respect. I earn love and respect by giving love and respect.

CONSCIOUSNESS AND SHARED REALITY

*The level of consciousness
is dependent upon what is
within a given soul.*

*Consciousness is a part of all that is
and is charged or forged
with individuality or free will.*

CHAPTER 2

CONSCIOUSNESS AND SHARED REALITY

How can we be lifted to higher consciousness? How do we achieve a renewed understanding and renewed life within this shared reality? Is it possible for God to lead us to our desired level of achievement on Earth? Within these sessions, souls come forth to speak on consciousness, thought, personality and free will within this shared reality. The souls also speak of the many bodies involved in evolution—each body independent, yet linked to all, and how the soul within the body is expressed. They speak of how thought creates each experience, and in fact, makes each experience what it is.

So, come sit with us.
These messages are meant for you.

(DICTATION BEGINS)

🌼 LEVEL OF CONSCIOUSNESS

Notebook #17, Page 5
This is a Wise One.

The level of consciousness is dependent upon what is within a given soul. Those thought processes, those personalities, those experiences, those memories, those resolves that integrate and form the color that makes up the observable beauty or dullness of the soul.

The integration process is a part of the Greater Self and is available for all to find. That portion of the Self that knows from where it came and where it is going and what the purpose for the soul portion is, that is in the reincarnational experience.

Partly it is there to learn and experience for its Self. This it can do alone, surviving, living in an ego-oriented three-dimensional world or portions of the Greater Self may become a part of that experience.

The Greater Self always wants to become a part of that experience so as to guide and mold the personality, so that the personality can more easily integrate into the whole Self that is the "whole" soul. In this way, the soul is uplifted to a greater consciousness of its Self and its relation to the shared reality and God.

Now the Greater Self can and does force its greater purpose on the portion in the human body. This is done in an effort to cancel a debt. In this way, the soul can be truly uplifted to a new consciousness. This accounts for a seeming desire and resolve, impulse, to suddenly do something that may be out of your Earthly character. Now there is always choice, a personality can deny that urge and not accept that debt. That is the nature of the learning and experience. It can evolve on Earth alone for the most part but will always return to the Greater Self for it has never really left.

Consciousness does indeed exist and there are levels of your consciousness that you will never become aware of. But it is there and is you and can reach you to the greatest heights or plunge you to the greatest depths. In infinite time, consciousness does indeed always exist. Now how one deals with consciousness is through thought. What you think forms you. One can seek through thought and action can or may come about. But the thought is always there forming its own energy. The thought exists in the shared reality and is accepted or rejected by individual consciousness with that shared reality.

The so-called evil that you say exists and can rightly point to humans on your Earth that "perpetrate that evil" is evil or just in the mind of the thinker. One would say, "how can that be right?" It is wrong to do this and in fact, if it is not beneficial to all then it certainly is not right. But in interpreting right and wrong, good and evil, one must realize who they are, where they are going, what they are doing and from whence they came. Start there and one will right many wrongs. Start there, for one is no more or less than the shared reality in which we all exist and the contribution we make becomes a part of not only the shared reality but of ourselves. Our Earth self, our greater selves, and the total shared reality of infinite consciousness in time.

Now in consciousness, one always has choices and makes those choices exploring probabilities through thought and action. That is where the expansion or contraction of consciousness emanates from. Is the choice a positive or a negative one? Is the choice a three-dimensional choice or a Greater Self-choice? The choice and the circumstances are always set by the individual soul just as the choice and the circumstances are always set by the portion of the soul, or you the human. Remember those conditions in which you live are a product of choice of the Greater Self and the human self. If you deny that, then go about changing your circumstances. The Greater Self will be there to guide and help you.

The consciousness of which I speak is you. Have no doubt of that. The choices or alternatives of which I speak are yours.

If you come to a road, you are faced with choosing to look for another, staying on the same road, or taking the road, and a whole set of other alternative choices are yours. But remember this, the roads are all within and the alternatives and choices are within. Understand that and you will greatly expand your consciousness.

Take the example of the child who seeking for the first time a Christmas tree, the wonder and excitement and all kinds of dreams, hopes, and desires spring forth. The child travels many roads through consciousness. Toys, Santa, Christianity, play, activity, human response to his gifts, food, family love, hope, desire, faith, believing, seeking, and the alternatives are multi-faceted, and any could bring forth action and another series of probable events.

Now thought is reality and the making of reality on Earth is through symbols. The example of a Christmas tree is very relevant to some, while the smell of baked bread, a picture or other symbols are relevant to others, each symbol representing a thought and stirring within the individual sets of other thoughts and symbols. But understand, the symbols and thoughts are created out of thought and are only as valid as you perceive them. In thought making, life making, symbol making, creating, ask "what is the purpose?" and understand it in terms of your defined purpose and accept it that way. If you are thought making, life making, symbol making, creating for others, then understand that you are working within shared reality with many different kinds of life consciousness that will perceive it in their own unique way. When dealing with man understand that mankind is a mass of individuality connected with greater selves, connected with God. Each forged with free will, each a part of the greater self and God, and God a part of all.

The way to reach each, to reach God, to understand shared reality, is from whence we all came—Love.

The consciousness does have what you on Earth would refer to as levels and for purpose of discussion and symbology, seven is an appropriate number. Many religions use this number in determining levels of achievement. I use the word "achievement" for in many situations it is measured as an achievement. That too is fine for symbology purposes. Many humans are geared just that way toward achievement and that is a fine motivator. However, there are some who feel like losers, the so-called "cards are stacked against them," and for them, an achievement approach may not be the best. In many cases, they are looking for that mind to change the direction of their lives. That divine

God, that superhuman who is going to lead them to achievement and happiness. What one must realize in infinite love, there is no achieving necessary, the love is right there. Within each exists their own personal God and it is the true God, for God is All.

Now if this is true, why does man not feel the presence of God within him? Why does not this presence move within him and tell him that I Am God and I am here for you? Why does not this Greater Self, guide one to this God? Why does one have these evil thoughts, these fears? Why is one blind, crippled, stutter, depressed and have negativity surround one? The reality is this, it is for you—your responsibility to begin; for you to make those necessary changes. Again, it is your choice and it is a matter of choice, and the choices are yours. By not making a choice and facing that question or fear within you, you make the choice.

Your father, mother, sister, brother, friend, confessor, idol, etc., cannot do it for you. Your God cannot do it for you.

The wonder of creation or the soul is that the soul as a part of God is forged with free will.

Now you feel lost, there is no one to help you, not even your God, and yet your God has helped you, has given you the greatest gift of love you can have, forged free will. That forged free will that for all is freedom no matter where you are, what your circumstances are. Slave or king, healthy or sick, within you, lies your future, past and present to guide, change and direct, for there are many ways for one to be reborn. You will have many lives and experiences here on Earth, but one can be reborn the moment the choice is made and pursued.

Wisdom is justice in your heart and understanding that justice in your heart is the justice you shall have.

The struggle is the battle. The battle is not with others but with ourselves. The battle is to overcome guilt and fear, understand that you have a right to human potential and that you are more and greater than you think you are. You have greater wisdom, more knowledge, and more personalities than you presently have. (Know) That God is available to you through you, that you are no more or no less than any other human on the Earth, that life is infinite, that God is infinite, that Love is all and the Word and the way.

None where lies this battle when you have been told, and think you believe and accept, what has just been said. If you accept and think about God's laws, you will practice them. This does not mean that you won't make mistakes, it means that you will not intentionally make mistakes or practice them. All that has been said is a battle and the battle is from within.

The battle is not war or violence. Righteousness and battle are not vindictive. Achievement is not the reward. Reward is not the achievement. It is the purpose, resolve, and endeavor, the understanding, compassion, and patience.

Through these, one will battle, will be righteous, will achieve, and will find the reward; the understanding what you are, where you are going, and from whence you came.

Total consciousness is, in reality, the total self and varies in meaning from soul to soul. The level of development or understanding within the soul is dependent on experience and the amount of structures. The soul builds with the self. Defining what is acceptable to the soul is a law of God for that is in keeping with forged free will. However, the definition is not necessarily accurate in terms of true reality in the perceiver though it may be and therefore it is. What is important to understand is that reality, energy, thought and love, exist forever. There are no conditions put upon truth. Truth is truth. From the single-celled energy to the multi-celled energy, all exist as part of the shared reality. To say that you are directly connected to animals, trees, elements, may seem startling and unacceptable but in shared reality, each contributes to infinite purpose and each is a part of thought. In tracing thought, we trace it to God, to all, for All is God and God is All. In total consciousness, each maintains its individuality and uniqueness while still being a part and a creation of thought.

The confusion of purpose exists in individual elements working in the evolutionary process of purpose—each battling and evolving toward understanding truth in their own unique way and not entirely accepting that each is a part of each and in love, the purpose is truth and in truth the purpose is love. In a sense, it is like one larger infinite organization that can work with each or work individually. In either situation, the working is part of the evolutionary process. The natural way is to work with each—that is the learned way—but that indeed is the battle to understand just that. Love is the clause—for in no other pure thought can one accomplish more. For in no other true thought can all accomplish more.

Thought consists of tiny impulses going through constant motion. Thought is ever vital and exists at all times. Thought contributes to all that is and is all. Random thought is just that and also exists. Matter (energy) that makes up the human is thought. Matter or energy are caused by thought and relate to thought. Random thought may or may not permeate certain forms of matter or the human. Thought forms the matter of the human body and can only meld with like-thought for greater energy or lesser energy. Example: A marble is a round object and hard and solid. A marble struck by a similar object does not permeate and become one but rebounds.

A marble though is also a mass of heated energy in a different form but still a marble in the making. However, it can be 10,000 or 100,000 marbles and be one. The marble may be a statue or a table and come from the same form or mass but evolving to a different form or mass.

A thought is like a marble in that it can be part of and melds into one idea or can be separate and different. It exists none-the-less and makes its contribution. In understanding that thought creates all, a major step in creating is reached. One can examine random thoughts and accept them as random thoughts picked from the matter of all integrated and restructured and extended out into all existence as another random thought. One can examine specific thought or create specific thought, direct those thoughts to specific energy masses which in turn can accept or reject, change or repeat. Each evolves individually and yet contributes to the mass. This is reality.

The thought of love is the universal thought. One thought is and can permeate all and the specific. The thought of love is the truth of all existence and thereby cannot be denied by an individual.

Consciousness is the total reality and thought forms consciousness. There have been past "religions" or statements or beliefs that relate to consciousness and this reality, like the Bible, men have also transcribed those thoughts into forms that were symbolic and acceptable.

This was done for the statement of the times. Mankind in relating to his physical environment structures beliefs that are acceptable or economically a beneficial idea. This is done out of greed much of the time. Mankind structures these beliefs to assume a position of power sometimes declaring that the knowledge only rests with a select few. Know this "knowledge is power;" how one uses that knowledge greatly influences mankind. How man accepts knowledge greatly influences mankind. Mankind at times in their history encourages knowledge and at other times discourages it.

Consciousness is justice in relation to contribution to all that is, in relation to each. Justice is consciousness contributing to the elevation of the total consciousness.

Consciousness relates to all forms of life even life that humans are not aware of. Consciousness is existence. Some existence is ordered, other existence is self-creating and evolving. Man is self-creating and evolving. Plants are an ordered existence following laws of nature that is part of Earth's planet. Plants are to provide food and beauty to forms of self-creating and evoking life. Animals are a form of man in a sense, for they were man in certain experiments that we have spoken. They were experimented with for a time as a form of experience and for that reason they were highly evolved in certain areas, namely communication. They, today, are still more aware of nature and its interrelation than man is. However, they are evolving as a separate set of soul experiences. The soul has many portions that are experiencing nature in different ways than the portion that you are experiencing.

✾ SOUL AND CONSCIOUSNESS

Notebook #19, Page 1
This is William Moore.

Consciousness is a part of all that is and is charged or forged with individuality or free will. Each element that is the soul is free to create and develop. The soul accumulates many experiences on Earth and other environments. The soul is certainly charged with individuality. The soul can create many experiences at once in terms of a human description. The soul can create these experiences simultaneously because there is no past, present, and future in true reality. The soul in creating develops separate but part of the essence or soul personalities. The personalities continue to develop after in earthly reincarnations.

This is Bill Bo.

The soul continues to have and hold these personalities as part of the essence. The soul develops these personalities and those personalities contribute and guide the extension of the soul in experience or other souls. It is a cooperative effort. This especially occurs in Earth's highly developed souls. They are the human elements that make major contributions to the Earth's creative force. Whether it be in art, politics, or religion the major contributions are made by a few rare personalities. These personalities have gained much from the Earth experience and the "in-between incarnation experience."

✿ THOUGHT AND CONSCIOUSNESS

Notebook #28, Page 4
This is a Wise One.

Each unit is valid and free will thinking and a part of love. Each unit is a thought converted to an image. So, each soul thought, or unit thought will have a life of its own but cannot be infinite until it is understood that it takes more than one unit to create anything of a lasting nature.

Consciousness is a thought that always was, is, and will be. Consciousness is that which always will create out of love, consciousness is a thought that is, was, and always will be. That which always will create out of love. That which cannot create for the self and must create for all and must endow all that is created with free will. All that is created, is created out of love's understanding of how new souls and forms of consciousness are always being created and living experiences through thought. This is the dream of consciousness and when one on Earth sleeps or meditates, one is closer to reality than when one is experiencing the experience. Thought creates each experience and in fact makes each experience what it is.

Now the new soul that is cast forth and forged with free will is at once closest to that creative force and at once furthest from that creative element. The new soul or consciousness element knows whereby it was created but does not understand. Knowledge is not understanding. The element, whether a soul reasoning or another order of consciousness, is through its very nature inclined to create and will create the element, by its own nature is free thinking and so long as the element is creating for all, it is indeed creating for the self and is creating love's beauty. When the element is creating for the self it is merely a perspective creativity that cannot live on infinitely. Now in the order of God, its order is love, free will, thought. These are the supreme truths that all elements come to understand. Elements must live enough experiences with all or many other orders to come to this truth. When that understanding comes about the element knows and is in what has been termed heaven. Heaven exists anywhere when that truth is lived and felt, understood, infinite grandeur, splendid understanding, indescribable happiness, and peace. Love is the greatest truth the supreme order of all.

WHERE CONSCIOUSNESS EXISTS

Wednesday, December 16, 1981, Session 74
This is a Wise One. We will now speak of consciousness.

Consciousness is thought. Thought is consciousness.

All that you see and experience is the thought of a greater consciousness of which you are part of. Consciousness exists at once being no past, present, or future. The probable consequence of thought is the future for the consciousness known as the soul.

When the soul is in tune with total consciousness and becomes a part of total consciousness there is renewed understanding, renewed life, just as when your personality's part of the greater essence integrates forming a new you. Consciousness, when righteous, never dies.

The clause of all including consciousness is love, that, of course, being essential and a part of consciousness. The love we speak of is not a love of man for a woman or a woman for a man, it is a love for all. When one is in total consciousness, one is in the natural state of love and creating.

Instincts that are part of ALL—ALL consciousness.

Now it is true that there are different species, shall we say of consciousness, plant, animal, and man, but all return to total consciousness, infinite consciousness.

To correlate the ideas of consciousness and your three-dimensional self simply record and monitor all your experiences in categories of: I create, I change, I accept, I do not understand, each item listed under those categories would tell one or two things.

First, a lot about the individual. Second, each item listed is the result of a thought. So, in the most basic example of everyday living, it becomes evident that thought creates the circumstance of three-dimensionality, just as thought created each soul.

We will now conclude and answer questions from either of you this evening.

Mike: Past, present, and future exist at once would it not be possible for one to attune himself to other vibrations and travel back in time?

Yes, but not the physical human body, but the ethereal body of the human or the soul body. And of course, the greater consciousness goes wherever that would occur.

Mike: Would the same be probable—future based upon thought but not the true future?

Even though difficult to explain, it is existing now through consciousness. What is existing now in consciousness is the words and actions and methods of future experiences just the so-called outline becomes consciousness has willed it so.

Mike: I have no more questions for now.

You may then go and relax.

❀ IDEA AND CREATIVITY

Sunday, February 28, 1982, Session 126
This is a Wise One.

In the creative reality, that which is created first begins as an idea. The idea is in the form of an image, the stronger the intent the more vivid the image. At the point of idea, it is merely a probability or an alternative.

Now ideas in truth exist as long as they are valid, necessary to the thinker. In the shared reality of existence, ideas are shared.

One selects from a myriad of probabilities and alternatives. Ideas are thought out, experiences rethought out and re-experienced. An idea is, therefore, a reality to those involved with that idea. It has no past, present, or future; it has validity, reality, experience, and probability, to the degree that those participating in that idea find it valid, necessary and generally rewarding.

Now all beings create in one manner or another. Creating is part of being. It is fine to rest and contemplate but the excitement of being is through creating. An idea is always a reality, and an idea has inherent within free will and probabilities that contain multidimensional aspects to them.

Ideas through experience created by the experience are more challenging in that they have rules, regulations, and stipulations guiding the idea within the experience.

Now the idea of love is in truth, reality. The idea of free will is in truth, reality. And the idea of thought is in truth, reality. However, perceived and defined within three-dimensional physical Earthly aspects in itself be colored, adjusted and adapted to circumstances—the idea that is.

So, to say to one "love is the truth and all are manifesting love in one degree or another and all have inherent free will and all is created by thought," true or untrue, to say these things without commitment, belief, desire, and on others within the experience is merely saying words. And of course, those words will always be perceived differently in a given point and an understanding within one's eternal development. That is all for tonight.

❀ EVOLUTIONARY SHARED REALITY

Tuesday, July 13, 1982, Session 204
We will now speak of shared reality. When evolution begins for a race, it begins at the beginning of one of many cycles. Evolutionary lines of development represent reflected thought that of course is projected by evolving souls and participated by evolving souls.

Now the reflection or projection of the soul will try and be itself as a reflected image until it realizes that it cannot, and is not destined nor does it want, to evolve alone. The soul may go through many experiences and this or these experiences follow orders and ordered and cyclic development. Now many physics and many transmissions have come from other realms and represent interpretation to greater and lesser degrees of evolution.

Experience is multidimensional as, of course, is thought.

Now within evolutionary lines within cycles, within experiences, there comes about the development of various structures that have come to be known as levels, steps, ladders, paths to something greater. Now the deities and gods that are sought, are represented in greater and lesser degrees by the aforementioned lines of development.

When a soul projects through the human personality, it, of course, creates a free will—freely evolving personality that will eventually find itself as part of a soul. Just as the soul will reorient itself through its order of development and ascend to a Godlike state. We will discuss that state more fully, but a simplistic statement: it represents the ultimate end, the process of thought, of love, and the handling of free will.

Now memories are within each projection of a soul based upon soul experience and learning and understanding.

Each of the aforementioned methods of finding something greater, be it heaven or be it God, first must experience their individual and personal dream of what heaven and God is, until they reach the level of awareness of being God.

Now some experience within a planet, some within a universe, some within seven universes, and some within 70 universes in the views continue multidimensionally on and on.

Evolution is always very personal for each element of God always possesses its individuality, realizing that one's individuality is contained within the *all*, requires great understanding. "Awareness" can be substituted for the word "understood," for it is completely natural, for breathing is natural, but not thought about, generally.

So rather, we say each teacher reflects in time, truth according to infinite understanding. This next age will reflect thought, love, free will, and reason. And yet reason drops away when a soul reaches the highly evolved state. Reason is only relevant where reason is needed.

This past age, shall we say the last 2,000 years or so, has reflected the awareness of supreme beings, the awareness of

something greater than the self. There are many lines of development in evolution that reflect or are reflected in, this most recent
2,000 years, in other cycles.

NEW AGE SHARED REALITY *(Same Session)*

The new age in one sense does reflect physical species' development for that development has a beginning and an end as you
know it now. And yet has infiniteness when it goes back into a
state of what you would refer to as electromagnetic fields. And
yet, no body can connect and coordinate into a new experience,
perhaps a new physicalness, and each soul that becomes a part
of that experience will focus into all orders of that experience.

This particular age, again, reflects certainly physical developments, certainly mankind's developments, and will even set
different standards of human and planetary developments. But
more importantly, it is a high spiritual age in which those incarnating will more fully practice to a greater and lesser degree and
more responsibility to greater and lesser degrees Godlike creating
and existing. Many older souls are participating in bringing about
this age of mankind and souls of lesser understanding would not
choose to participate. No more than the human who is not trained
as a surgeon would do more than take a few pills to correct an
illness. The analogy being the experience would not be construc-
tive for any of those involved. There, of course, can be numerous
analogies to support this.

Now each line of developments and methods of evolution or
paths is valid and true. And none represent more than truth.
Some lines of development are more highly specialized in a particular and logical perspective and some in other areas. But none
represent more than the evolutionary understanding of truth.

That will conclude for this evening.

SOUL IN THIS SHARED REALITY

Sunday, September 19, 1982, Session 239
This is a Wise One.

Each universe represents a system that souls enter to evolve
through. Earth's universe is one of seven universes that rotate

around a nucleus of energy and mass. And these seven and the nucleus rotate around another system. Creation and evolution are a part of the soul within all systems in truth, and truth is God. Within each element of a system is truth, and truth is God. God is thought, will, and love. Through love, the highest, the purest, the most truthful thought God gave, God's will, is to give and to create in God's likeness.

Now each system has sets of physical properties defined there as vibration and color. Within the physical properties, there are laws and cycles of operation. Everything within the system is set within a cycle to give order to the system, to give justice to the system, to give evolvement in an ever-expanding and contracting reality.

There are processes within the system of your universe that will never be humanly known. There are processes within the soul's mind system that will never be known by the soul as an individual evolving element of God. Such knowledge and such wisdom and understanding come when the individual becomes part of the whole.

When souls are evolving, whether they recognize they are part of a whole and shared reality or not, there is an interrelationship that cannot be measured through individual observation.

A set of systems is not a part of truth. Like a machine upon Earth, there was and is and will be thought that creates, operates, and dismantles the system or machine. The thought operation behind the machine makes the machine. Thought has quality and will to it. In the physical world what is made is undone in a like manner, thought manner.

That is all for this evening.

Tuesday, April 18, 1982, Session 172
This is your Wise Guide.

When the soul is evolving within shared reality of allness, consciousness, beingness, as on Earth—so it is within the realms and degrees of soulness—there exist vibrational and frequency differences that evolving souls perceive as something more than themselves and as realms of the unknown.

The multidimensional aspect of thought, free will, love, creation, evolution, order, justice, and infinity, is an ever-changing, expanding, pulsating, cyclic reality that is guided by individual perception (soul, element, projection, perceptive point reality) that functions within the tenets and reality of truth, which permeates all.

Now there are some evolving elements of God and all that are unaware of the ordered reality of other evolving lines of development. But God has bestowed upon the smallest element, however, defined and limited by order, that truth which transcends and permeates all and that is love given.

Here is a simple statement. If one reading this book contained natural impulses within themselves, they would destroy from within that element to some degree. This is also inherent within any energy field. Now, if one is projecting and giving, there is a natural law that exists whereby one will receive back what one has given. This extends into any and all experience. Now if one gives love for another it is returned and regenerated to others. If one gives for another for the self, it too will be returning but not regenerated for another. Therefore, if there are ten people standing in a room and each did everything only for the self, then ten people would eventually diminish their creative and energy potentials. If five were male and five were female eventually this race of ten people would perish for they lived only for the self. If they choose to share and build, then the race would grow with some ebb and flow but continue to grow and reproduce and recreate.

When the soul projects within experience it projects within an order, species, as a free will, freely-evolving portion of itself and God, and becomes part of an evolutionary chain or line of development evolving to an understanding of the species and the order.

No line or order of development completely dies within the allies of all's thought and can be reestablished, reexperienced at any chosen time within evolutionary processes.

The soul or fragment or projection in the process of experiencing or fulfilling that experience to its potential need only be truthful to the self, that beingness, that is within all and *just* development will occur.

The soul, whatever is decided, however many cycles, however many experiences it takes, will create its own method through attitude of finding eternal peace. But throughout all experience, soul has the, sometimes, hidden potential of changing and choosing the paths and roads to understand truth and God. There are many paths if the soul wishes to take the bumpy road of hard knocks, it is but an excursion from the main highway of truth. And to get back to the highway, one must travel back through the bumpy road. Many such excursions are taken, the process of reaching that destination called "truth." The destination is the same. The free will choice exists within each to choose how they wish to reach that destination.

Now the soul intuitively and intrinsically knows its destination and that is God and Truth. However, like the travelers on the road of life, if in error or by one's current placement and perspective in life, one takes the wrong road, one must travel back over that road to find the true path. In a sense that is not just logical but justice if many wrong paths are taken and the trip back is that much harder. Now when traveling back to the road of truth you will come upon the same obstacles that you met when you first chose that path and ever created that path. If you face these obstacles and find your way back to the main road of truth, you will find peaceful traveling that much sooner. Now you will travel again over all the paths you have created.

The paths and highways of experience of life, each excursion is represented by intent. That will conclude for this evening.

❀ OUR VARIOUS BODIES IN THIS SHARED REALITY

Friday, October 22, 1982, Session 252
This is a Wise One.

There are many bodies involved in evolution. There is the human body or other orders of physical nature. There is the soul body, there is the personality body, there is the Divine body. Each body is independent and yet linked to all. Each body is a reflection of greater thought. Each body through will is and can separate. The soul body is that which is focused about the human and known as an aura. The personality is focused within the body and shines from within the body. The spiritual body is within and out of a body. The bodies reflect the thoughts.

Thoughts guide all and are marked by color, vibration, and sound. In evolution, the colors change through thought. In wisdom and truth, the bodies are all connected to the focus point in one manner or another, linked with a cord that runs to and through the coordination point within an evolving system. Now this cord, for lack of a better word, is running hither and to the space, some of it visible, some of it not.

The bodies can move about and function within vibratory levels of like bodies. High vibrations can function within each lower vibration. The reverse is too true. These bodies can be in many places at once. Bodies are mobile and can assume the shape that the thought brings into being. Bodies will mingle together. The bodies can be any shape but the personality body will assume many times the shape, approximately, of the most recent physical body.

Wisdom is attained by assembling a cord in like-thinking. When thoughts are being projected with intent, there is an un-assimilating of the cord. When thoughts are being received the same is true. The cord is then in what can best be described as sections and there are many cords within and without each other depending upon vibration. The cord carries impulses. The cord of truth-life is within all and is connected to all evolving worlds and systems. It is not measured by sound or color, it is beyond that description. Now is it measured by form or substance?

The cord of life is what is known as life's "stream." It forms and is all. It is within and without all systems. Now there are cords within cords. Now each thought is projected, remains alive forever and is connected to a cord that is part of an energy source of a body. The cords, like roots, connect in likeness and form energy fields and coordination points, forming large masses of energy. A cord then carries with it, impulses of thoughts. Now the being thinking will receive some mixture because of the nature of cords. Analogically speaking, the human body is made up of systems that are blood, air and water, nitrogen, hydrogen, that form masses that are cells that have bones, flesh, organs, to carry the air, and blood and water within the body. Body comes together and apart in the physical order. But behind this body lies many thoughts that went in to create it. Behind all thought is God the creator of all. As the soul evolves it finds greater communication with increased frequency, for lack of a better word, ascends to higher vibratory levels and becomes more in communication with all that it is. And the soul reaches a God-like state, is beyond a universal type description, but comes in contact with the light force of all.

The cord of eternal life cannot be found except through the path of eternal truth. The cord is not found through seeking. It is beyond seeking. It is found through letting go and accepting.

Quietly comes the truth. A thought for the infinite special. The creator is in each, so each is both created and creator placed in time.

That is the "I Am" the mind of minds.

Each may and will come to be that mind in truth when the unfoldment and truth are understood. Then the awareness and understanding that the separation was but a dream, becomes I Am. The truth is not taught by another, though another for a time may lead you to that truth. You know where you are and what you need. There is a time that you can no longer struggle for your answer but must just be and accept, so the answer may unfold.

The cord of which we speak is often referred to in literature without the real meaning behind it. In thought, impulses are carried to and through various vibrations. There is a network of web-like cords that carry the impulses. This is connected to cords that go beyond the realm of evolution. Suffice to say, eternity is forever and thought and mind is forever. The cords are like then swaying in the wind, bending to the tune of the vibrational thought. That that is between and in and is the cord of love. Love is the gap and link between all vibrations.

That completes this section on the cord of life. Yes, some carry messages in certain directions so to speak or carry certain quality of vibration of messages.

SOUL

*God created Soul out
of the light of Love.*

*God thought, and the soul came into being.
The thought was love; the soul was
forged with love's free will.*

CHAPTER 3

SOUL

Who are we as Soul? Why did we choose to come into this life? What is our individual soul's purpose on Earth? How does our God-given free will relate to our Earthly purpose and our soul's advancement? Discover the truth of existence, as expressed by many souls in the following sessions, and what we, as Soul, know before entering into human form. In this fascinating chapter, you will explore sessions that have the power to positively shift your perspective of your own existence and create a greater connection with and understanding of those with which you share this Earthly experience, as well as remind you of your divine connection with God.

So, come sit with us.
These messages are meant for you.

(DICTATION BEGINS)

✿ SOUL WAS CREATED

Notebook #10
This is your Wise Guide.

God created soul out of the thought of love *(the light of love)*. Soul is a thought of love. God created the energy out of a thought of love. The energy is a thought of love. God created *energy* as a form for the soul, for God is total energy. *Energy* is a sound converted into color.

All are part of the creative evolutionary process. God is All. All is God.

God created all energy and is all energy. Energy is of love, the thought, soul, sound, and color. Energy is the continuing creative process by which all continue to create. Energy is that which creates and holds together your world, your solar system. When the soul no longer desires a solar system, such as Earth and its planets on which to experience, then it will disappear just as quickly as it was made to appear.

Notebook #29, Page 17
This is a Wise One. We will now speak of soul.

The soul is a reflection of God or All That Is. God created the soul out of infinite love. Out of infinite love, the soul has been forged with free will. God thought, and the soul came into being. The thought was love; the soul was forged with love's free will. God is and always has been. The soul is a love of God and is always a part of God. God loves all that has been created and all that has been created has been created equally. God has willed that through love forged free will; that which the soul creates shall be the soul's just reward. Therefore, that which is thought shall be the soul reality and justice. The soul is always infinite and forever. The soul in its true state is a love seeker for love is at the seed of all souls.

The souls that are born out of God's thought of love and that are forged with good free will are a thought reflection of God and are marked with color.

Color is the visual form that marks souls. White is the pure color of love and exists to some degree within all. Black is the marking of "love held closely," is self-love only. Black alone cannot exist forever. Green is the color of learned experience and becomes a part of all souls.

Red is the color of emotion that is uncontrolled and is physical. Blue is the color of emotion that is controlled. Yellow is the color of God's emotion. Yellow has white, yellow has green. Yellow has blue. The yellow that is a reflection of all of these, is a bright, sparkling, beautiful gold. All colors form to make a reflected image and a reflected image is a reflected thought of the soul. God does exist, and God is All. Those that are of God and love given are known throughout Earth's love as Gods and heavenly beings and are "interpreted in various manners that reflect a physical manifestation and hope." God forms all and all are formed by 'thought'—that thought is love given and all are forged with free will.

All are created equally in the eyes of God and God loves all equally. God has willed that none shall perish who do not want to perish, and that created out of love given, which is All, shall never perish, for it is not in their infinite desire for selfhood.

God accomplished physical reality and all reality through thought and image and that image gains a reality through vibration that is accomplished through acceleration, velocity, and frequency. All thought is ever present and ever creative and everchanging and ever learning; all thought exists without a past, present, and a future and with a past, present, and a future, a time and no time. It exists as visualization and reality and probability. The visualization is the past, present, and future; the reality is the present and the probability is the future.

All form the reality of time and all exist at once through a method of sound marked by color, the sound, of course, being frequency, the color being a reflective of thought. God has infinite thoughts of love and infinite thoughts of love are the only truth.

Now love has two sides and within those sides exists infinite learning, seeking, experiencing, understanding, and exploring, that have multidimensional realities. Love given and love held closely. Love given has an ever-expanding and creative and happy/free effect. Love held closely, has a constraining structural effect with inherent structures and limitations which bind with structure through fear. All is soul created and all is a part of the infinite reality of God.

The truth of existence is thought, love, and free will. That is the supreme truth. It is reflected in all concepts of God and belief. It is manifested in a variety of learned ways within all realities including the physical. All realities are a part of God and God is a part of all realities. Truth is a part of all realities, however, reflected truth is not always recognized. Love, thought, and free will, are the only truth and they exist in each element of God and all. For God is Love, God is Each and God is All.

Sunday, March 14, 1982, Session 136
They are ready to begin.

This is a Wise One.

When the soul is given life or created, the method by which this occurs is through thought visualization in creation of the soul, it is an expression of God. Like a personality is a part of the soul, the soul is a part of its creator and the soul's creator is God.

To create a soul can only be done by completely understanding thought, love and free will. For all of those, the thought, love, and free will are an inherent part of every soul.

Therefore, the notion that all upon Earth are created by a supreme being is valid and true. For out of the supreme thought of love, souls were created and forged with free will. Each soul has inherent within it the God-given talent of creating. What souls cannot be given is understanding, for understanding comes about by not just observing but doing. Not just doing correctly, but erroring.

There are countless other experiences that the soul, through eternal beingness, lives. For a soul as God loves to be free, loves to be loved, loves to create. A soul sleeping creates sleep, idle contained thoughts and accomplishes no growth for fulfillment.

Better to live, express, love, error, and do, then to rest in anxiety, wishing, hoping, yearning, yet contained and restricted by inner anxiety from expressing.

We will conclude for tonight and leave both of you with something we wish you to think on—free will. That is all for this evening you may go now.

Thursday, March 25, 1982, Session 144

This is your Wise Guide.

The soul, when it is in the process of transferring to Earth a portion of itself, of projecting a portion of itself, does so through thought and form change. This requires a form of meditation whereby the soul creates an image that has a slower vibratory form. Now, this relates to the transfer of the created personality that will inhabit the physical body. The body is genetically created and takes with it inherited characteristics that make up the physical. Even the evolutionary process of creating the human body requires molecules, cells, and chemicals, which form a part of God as all does. These are orders within orders, as each projection and portion of God is.

Now the physical form that the personality will inhabit is known to the soul before it projects into the body. There is study before entering the body, you see. The physical forms related to the physical body through what Earth calls conception. The physical evolution of the body relates to justice, evolution, love, and thought. The body will give what it is given and evolve into certain probable physical selves through the process of thought evolution, experience, justice, and love. Love can and does change all.

NEW SOULS

Wednesday, April 21, 1982, Session 158

This is a Wise One.

When the soul is first created, the soul is visualized from a supreme creative force. Supreme in the fact that it is a highly evolved truth-bearing consciousness that is the God of All.

This supreme consciousness is itself multidimensional and infinite, understanding in practicing all of God's infinite laws without creating negative justice. When the visualization occurs, there is a new soul that grows in form and understanding. The best analogy that one can refer to is a child being born and raised. Now new souls are instructed and know of God's truths but like a child who is raised with certain beliefs, understanding what one already knows requires experience, experience requires doing.

Now the soul like a child is guided by those souls that have created this new soul. All such creations are infinite. When a new soul decides to experience, it is sent off, so to speak, to various schools of learning and frameworks of learning. Eventually, the soul will try its hand at experiencing.

New souls experience through visualization and thought projection. A personality fragment created from a greater self is the soul's reflection in psychological time and experience.

Through thought of love, this soul was created, possessed of free will with an inherent need to express love and an inherent need to create. Those creating souls through infinite understanding guide and direct but cannot tamper or send the will of another. Now an understanding of balance and flow of the shared reality are at such a supreme state that new souls who know this are at times reluctant to openly express and create out of concern of error.

However, wisdom dictates, or rather, guides that understanding, comes through the use of one's inherent free will as well as through the use of thought or love. In the soul's greatest sense of being and reality there exists that not yet understood, a grand indescribable need to give love. For inherent in the soul is the knowledge that to express and to give love is to receive love.

However, the use and application of love, thought, and free will, implies wisdom that follows patterns of unfoldment whereby the soul expresses over time, space, and distance, through a multifaceted and multidimensional order, diffusion of expression. One of those orders is what many focused within the reality of the Earth's solar experience.

So, to gain a glimpse of the magnitude and power of a soul in its most loving state, that beingness is dispersed over infinite orders of which the Earth's entire system is just one. Within each "solar order" exists a semi-infinite number of orders that the "great soul" also expresses over.

Now each manifested expression of the "great soul" contains an inherent right of freely evolving creative expression. This expression is paradoxical in nature when perceived from the viewpoint of the thought projection on the experiencing soul, in that one in any reality or circumstance is only as free as one is willing to express and only as confined as one is constrained from expressing. To express is to give and receive, to constrain is to limit. To express implies through God's laws of infinite wisdom just loving, and just receiving through any ordered experience.

The infinite reality is the greatest is God and the least is God. All is God. Yet the greatest shall see the least and the least shall be the greatest. For what God had given so shall God receive.

God gives to all and all give to God.

God is Love. Love is God. God is All. All is God.

In all human endeavor does not the child or the stranger comfort and understand and do they not discover that love is the greatest comfort and understanding. Love is all. All is love. God is love. Love is God.

✿ ENERGY IN ALL CREATIONS

Sunday, August 22, 1982, Session 223
This is a Wise One.

Energy is formed by thought. Energy is formed through sound. Sound is formed through speed vibration. When a soul is created a visualization is projected into a reality. What has been said about God creating for companionship is summed up in the word "love given," for one has to give to receive. This soul is mind unto itself. It is self-unlearned.

Ancient philosophies have spoken of end for this soul when it returns. What is meant by that is an end of falseness, an end of unfulfillments, an end of fear and guilt and wonder about the nature of itself?

Upon creation, a soul possesses the ability to create and knows not how to use the ability. The soul feels loved and knows it is loved. And for a time or no time depending upon the perspective, it remains in the comfort of that love. And yet the nature of a soul is to understand the self, something that can only occur through experience.

There are many experiences for the soul, many. There is one God that creates all from pure love.

When the soul returns to God, the creator of all, it is a seasoned soul ready to co-create.

Energy is in all creations. When energy, which is formed from the mind, enters any reality or learning environment it understands or rather is aware that it is set within a framework of development. However, the soul has guides that are always with the soul.

The soul only enters a chosen framework after becoming aware of its creative abilities and wishing to create. With guidance, the soul will focus into a framework reality and will focus within all orders of the framework.

The soul evolves through each order and each framework and projects within the limitations of that framework which is made up of many orders.

When the soul understands its nature, it will evolve into other frameworks. Infinite is infinite and souls are created always. Very simply, when a soul comes to understand, the soul then enters an elevated stage of God development and works as a learning co-creator having satisfied the soul self that God is the only truth, not the self. As a God or God imitator, shall we say, this soul goes through a season of creating out of love and learning and aiding other souls. The soul always has available recorded within its soul mind all experiences and memories. When the soul leaves a framework, the soul leaves those memories within the soul self but deeply buried.

Marcellas are creating for the purpose of transitioning into the season of truth. Energy is vibration and visual matter within various vibrational realities. That is all for this evening.

✿ WHAT SOULS ARE

Friday, September 25, 1981, Session 5
This is William Moore.

Souls are free spirits, souls are parts of all that is and all that is—is God. God is All and All is God. Souls do form alliances. We are all—all in an alliance. Groups of souls do form an alliance for a purpose. The purpose is always, always, love.

In the beginning, there was God and Love and Love is God and God is All and All is God. Souls evolved and grew to understand that those tenets, that love is God and God is Love and All is God and God is All.

Souls have free will and go through various experiences and reincarnations here and many other places.

This is Edgar Cayce. Souls go through various learning here, Earth, their Earth, and many other learning places and environments. Souls having free will to choose those experiences.

Wednesday, June 2, 1982, Session 179
This is a Wise One.

The soul is a creation of God's supreme intelligence. God's supreme intelligence who creates worlds and experiences and contributes to worlds and experiences, are worlds and creators, and permeate within worlds experiences and systems as wisdom, creators, lovers, and guides, of the experiential direction for the cycles and evolutions of souls. Experience is within various frequencies and dimensions, for souls are infinite.

A soul is created into an experience, more than one experience, for at the beginning of infinity was infinity and all returned to infinity. There are certain wisdoms and truths that are infinite, cannot and will not be destroyed. They manifest the ultimate and creative power, know all, see all, and go forth without fear. They are Gods, I Am, supreme intelligence, that which represents the highest attainment of truth.

Truth functions and permeates all experience in all dimensions. Vibration, color, frequency, is within all experience and reflects the creative elements of soulness which contribute to, in degree, God and all.

When Gods create there is a process of visualization that through modes of time becomes reality. The Gods through visualization of a God-mind understand, understand what the beginning and the end of a given experience is. Souls that do not fulfill their destiny within the realm of that experience focus and develop within other experiences.

We will conclude for this evening.

✿ ORDERS AND FRAGMENTS WITHIN THE SOUL

Wednesday, July 7, 1982, Session 201
This is a Wise One.

The soul is itself comprised of ordered elements and each ordered element is comprised of fragments/portions of experience and each fragment of experience lives forever as a memory within the soul ordered element; and each ordered element lives forever within the soul.

In total, the soul exists forever through evolution to understand truth. Truth is possessed by every thought projection for evolutionary purposes, maintaining eternal validity by possessing thought, ordered free will and love.

Each element, fragment, order, soul, and all create, and were, and are, created by thought, marked by color.

Thought is energy and creates energy. Energy is vibrational in nature and marked by color. What matters is not that one accepts certain theories or rejects them, it is that one comes to an internal understanding and creates and lives and exists and functions as God intends.

That is all for this evening.

Thursday, July 29, 1982, Session 210
This is a Wise One.

A soul upon entering any reality is at once given free will, is at once possessed of thought, and has love at the core of their thought being. The soul extends fragments *(portions of itself)* into orders. The soul, through order, experiences by projecting images into an already created physical or like-experience. The soul does this with guidance and help.

Other developmental experiences are as guides, teachers, harmonizers, speakers, and a variety of others. Each performs within their own realm as a method of coming to understanding.

Each area that is entered for development has its own perspectives, realities, structures, and understandings. Each is unique and yet bound together with all others in that reality, just as all are bound together in God's total reality.

The soul focusing in various realities does so than with help, aide, and assistance.

That will conclude for this evening. 10:59 P.M.

Tuesday, October 26, 1982, Session 256
This is a Wise One.

The soul is multidimensional, as thought is multidimensional. The will of the soul is such that it projects into experience until it learns enough about itself to understand that it is not singular in nature and not an island unto itself but part of all that is and all that is, is God. The soul projects through thought in an ordered manner focusing into all orders in the mind of the soul at once.

The soul fragments then enter into all orders and knows not itself except that it is and it's something greater than itself exist. Now the nature of order changes over the physical cycles of physical worlds. The experience is the same and yet different. The worlds may be different but the purpose behind the experience is the same. To find that creator that is the creator of all, souls begin a journey of thought projecting through ordered fragments of themselves. But each creation is created like unto the laws of God possessed of free will, possessed of thought, and possessed of love. The souls focus and experience various exposures to life.

The soul travels a journey of the mind not focused within physical time but focused within the mind's time which is always now. The soul as thought or mind is a mass of energy that can assume any shape it wishes. The soul itself as thought and energy evolves at various different levels. In the mind of the soul, it experiences based upon perception for until it completely understands that it is not meant to be individual but is meant to be a part of all. The mind of the soul recognizes then that there are other souls about them. And that it is a basic perception upon where it is currently focused.

Now through God and truth, all are possessed of truth and the same innate abilities. However, upon making the decision, the choice to test itself, the soul leaves memory of what it was and perceives from a focused perception. In other words, the soul, like each thought of existence, is focused in time. And the time is always now in the mind of the soul. And each thought will carry within it innate truths that all possess.

Now when a soul is at a point of perception and time it is giving off energy and thought at a vibrational level. This form of energy relates to and exists because of and has thought. And is not touched or moved by anything other than thought and that which is within its vibrational level.

When the soul projects thoughts, those thoughts remain with the soul forever until they are no longer necessary or valid and become so understood that they are both a part of a soul and no longer a part of a soul. This is a form of energy that is pure. An example might be the soul's study of jealousy or envy. It might focus within various different experiences and create a being in that experience that possesses thought, love, and will like the soul, but is focused within that vibrational level of experience.

When the soul has experienced enough to understand, then jealousy disappears, is no longer needed to experience. Those thoughts remain forever locked into a vibrational level seeking other thoughts as forms of energy and vibrate and remain within this level of vibration until it can no longer find like-energy patterns and it has energy changes, vibration, and dissolves more slowly and more slowly until it finds like-energy sources in which to move about more freely.

Now the soul that we speak of one must remember is a fragment of a greater soul self and entered an evolutionary cycle of many orders. And the experiences that are related to the human order, for in other orders, jealousy may not be what is to be learned. And what is to be learned within all orders is that there is God, the creator of all. When the soul is discovering itself, when the fragmented soul is discovering itself, it knows this yet does not fully understand it. It's always aware that there is something greater than itself but does not yet understand it.

We will conclude for this evening.

❀ IN THE DREAM WORLD (Same Session)

(My father must have told them of a dream he had; I thought their response was of value to you because it touches on the importance of learning through nightly dreams, so I have included this short section.)

We will now interpret any portion of your dream. The general intent of your dream was symbolic in nature; in the dream world, there are many realities. The soul or greater self is aware of at its particular vibrational level. These realities are interpreted for they change. The best manner of presenting these, many times is, through symbology and visualization. You are currently going through chaos and turmoil for you are shifting for a level of awareness. Inner change always brings about confusion, illusion, new fears, new doubts. As you continue your journey, understanding will unfold and you will see fears drop away. Some spend a whole lifetime. Some find a measure of peace within an experience. Some do both. You are on the right track headed in the right direction and the peace that you find will come to more closely align yourself in God's will, which is manifested in the word, and the word is love expressed in a variety of ways. But always intuitively best as you, the individual, understands.

Have a good evening and pleasant dreams.

❀ NATURE OF SOUL

Thursday, December 17, 1981, Session 75
This is your Wise Guide.

The nature of the soul is such that when the soul is born out of love and forged with free will, it is born with basic instincts of love and creating.

The creating out of love is the goal and when a soul manifests a personality in the Earth's sphere, the personality is too forged with free will. Now, this may be more than one personality at a time. Now there is always a greater consciousness outside of Earth's sphere. There is the greater individual soul for each fragment belonging to that soul and there is infinite loving consciousness.

Now when personality departs the human body and returns, it is greeted by friends and loved ones, and when upon gaining some form of reuniting with the greater self, a decision about reincarnating will exist within that soul and that soul may choose to reincarnate and learn, taking with it any lessons from their teachings.

When the soul finally accepts all the individual personalities, then truth is achieved and the necessity of incarnating on Earth is achieved. At that time, they will have gone through many incarnations on Earth and live the justice of reincarnation and begin to reap the fruits of their labor.

We will conclude that statement for this evening.

❀ SOUL BETWEEN INCARNATIONS

Monday, February 22, 1982, Session 121

I AM THAT I AM. When the 'personality' is between incarnations it continues to gain experience, to rest and relax, to create, for the most part, without the stress of human personality. There are exceptions for those souls who create stressful situations. They are not aware that they are doing this. They are just aware that they are no longer on Earth and essentially pick up where they left off. Souls gather in groups of like souls. And as they become more understanding they simply shift to another group of like understanding. Now the reason for the description, various levels, is for those souls and humans who find a structure beneficial. When a soul becomes more enlightened the soul may aide other souls and may shift from (quote-unquote) "one level to another."

The soul upon recognizing their greater self will bind together and begin to gain more understanding. When the souls between lives form other experiences, those experiences can take place in almost any setting. Some find it beneficial to pursue experiences in other settings before reincarnating back on Earth. The justice of the Earth's incarnation is not affected by these other experiences though God's Universal Laws apply in all experience.

Some souls between incarnations are aides, some teachers, students, some act as guides for souls first leaving the Earths experience. When the souls first transfer back to the Earth's experience, they, of course, chose time, birth, and circumstance of their entry and are a new fledgling personality with memories connecting back to other experiences.

The multidimensional aspect of the soul's evolution applies both on Earth and after Earth. The soul assumes a form that is most appealing to the soul, many times it is from the previous incarnation. Souls who reincarnate have guidance from wiser ones because of the multidimensional aspect. Of evolution and of experience there are in truth a multitude of paths to God.

Those philosophical religions who structure the paths do so for three-dimensional perceptions.

The soul is like a crystal ball, spinning, reflecting various colors, hues, shades. The colors change, the positions change, the look changes, therefore, the crystal ball changes, so too with the soul that is constantly experiencing backward and forward every which way the evolutionary process of understanding love given.

Now, various books attribute and describe levels; these again are structural.

Mike is sleeping and snoring!

He is awake now. That was quick.

When the soul is gathering these various experiences, it is seeking and finding a level of understanding whereby the soul feels comfortable.

Whatever the form or the shape or the experience, all function according to the laws of God. All function based upon the laws of love, however, the perception or being of the soul must first be recognized individually.

There are some wise souls, highly elevated, who believe that the mind, the thought is all, and some who believe free will and others who believe love. All are equal and necessary. For thinking and creating cannot exist without following laws of love. And the thinking and creating can only create free will thoughts. The love cannot exist without the thought or the free will endeavor and the free will cannot function and exist without a thought and following the principles of love. They are equally and finally and always dependent upon each other.

Love, thought, and free will, is the truth of being, all being. Love, thought, free will, is God. And all, ALL is God and God is ALL. All is thought and thought is all. All is free will and free will is all. All is love and love is all. God, love, free will, are truth.

Are there any questions?

Mike: No, I have no questions.

Then I bid you a good evening.

Mike is shaking—and mouth movements—but I can't hear anything.

Notebook #32, Page 10

This is a Wise One.

When the soul is between earthly lives or between experiences, wherever that experience is taking place, the soul is a just understander of their own development. Justice is learned and studied until there is an acceptance within the soul as to the chosen method of resolving inner conflict.

Within the soul, there is sometimes inner conflict that is based upon a lack of understanding of the soul's natural evolution. This lack of understanding is of course resolved through just experience (karma). When the soul is between lives, there is a much more relaxed and yet studious method of resolving inner soul conflicts. The approach is learned based upon experience by like souls and teachers of wisdom.

The Guides are, too, learning and learn with Earthly souls. Guides sometimes have experienced Earthly lives and sometimes choose to guide before entering Earthly life. Guides are a few souls that have learned the principles of soul evolvement and are excellent teachers but have not generally experienced the Earth's reincarnational experience.

The soul is then always aided by its greater self and guides in their experience on Earth. Now the soul, between Earth's experience, is as was said in study as to its nature and to like-soul nature. But soul between lives realizes that there is more wisdom and perceived other levels of development. The soul seeks to understand that evolutionary advancement.

Now soul can follow many paths of development through intent and doing by just observing the path is longer. The paths that are followed are recognized by the soul as self-advancement, soul-advancement, and shared-advancement. When souls are on the path of advancement they are not always upon an understanding of truth but are learning to understand other aspects and creative realities of the soul nature. Therefore, when those upon Earth speak of spirit wars and good and evil and heaven they are speaking of terms of the paradox of love. Love given and love held closely. Both are paths to understanding and both paths are traveled by the advancing soul.

However, to travel, one exclusively can only say what that path is. It does not say what the other path is not.

When the soul is between lives, the soul will indeed travel to many different dimensions in seeking both experience and understanding. The soul that becomes more evolved or is more of an adventuresome soul will do this often between lives as a learning tool. The soul will often travel with like-souls or souls that are what Earth would call friends or relatives. Plans are often made, and dramas are often created and lived. These dramas are sometimes projected to the Earth experience.

The soul will endeavor to find what the best method is of expressing and having an experience that has purpose, justice, creatively or merely observation. The soul is a lover of companionship and that is a need by all souls to some degree. The companionship can be to share and receive or to use and gain personally. The reasons why many souls seek an Earth-like experience are of course varied, but an Earth-like experience provides more opportunity for growth in that there are those structural limitations that are inherent with the physical domain.

The soul that is expressing for the self only is likely to choose the Earth experience for personal gain and enjoys this experience for a while, while on Earth. That same soul will not find the same challenge within the expansiveness of in-between lives experience because of the freedom that is enjoyed between lives and the lack of controls that one soul has over another. God's laws are in effect between lives and souls knowingly hurt themselves by going against God's laws.

The soul between lives in a multidimensional experience, the soul will be a great artist, will study, record a soul behavior, will create great events of creativity, will aid other souls in soul development or various other multidimensional pursuits and activities. The pursuit of these activities is up to the soul and the methods and applications of pursuit are up to the soul.

The vastness of creativity and the mind and love is ever expanding and very fulfilling. The most creative souls are those souls that have the greatest understanding of God's operational laws. Now one reason why not all souls are aware of these laws is for essentially the same reason the humans are not aware of these laws in specific. Through developmental evolution and learning laws that are most applicable to the individual of group soul's development. Souls place limitations upon themselves in regard to this learning and evolutionary process to just learn and know what God's laws are not enough.

To understand how they apply, why they apply, when they apply, where they apply, can best be gained by experience.

Now we are speaking of between lives of course and not the Earth experience for that will be covered at another time.

The nature of the soul is such that when there is a focusing of energy, there is a justice that is being melded. The soul that focuses and creates a personality or being is doing so to experience and learn, and practice creating, and justice. The focusing is a method of creating, and inherent in all creating is, all that is created is forged with free will. When focusing on Earth, free will is inherent in all of God's creations. All of God's creations can choose their life and their death within the constraints of order and justice.

Souls focused, or rather portions of souls focused within experience, all create through expressions of love. All elements respond to love. Love, however, is perceived differently by each element and for that matter each soul. For through free will and other experience, it is different for each element of God.

The realization and understanding of love given, thought, and free will, is by souls that have evolved to a higher state of understanding. However, though this is a truth of God and a reality of experience and being, perceptions and understandings will still be different for evolving souls. For each soul by its learning nature is building structures and frameworks by which to learn and experience. When the soul has experienced and learned the Earth's experience the soul is free to no longer use Earth as a focal point of experience. Some souls do return though for a purpose of sharing their vision with all.

HOW SOUL COMMUNICATES

Saturday, March 20, 1982, Session 140
This is a Wise One.

We will now write for the book. When the soul is communicating with other souls it is done through thought. When the soul is communicating with other souls it is done through a process of electromagnetic transference of thought or impulses.

Where the two can be connected one can speak through a human (for example). Now in the dream state thoughts of intent are accomplished the same way. Within each soul and each portion exists a connection that is separated only by frequency.

Now depending upon mind element within the fragment, communications through impulse are many times done through visualization.

Now that visualization is triggered to become apparent to the receiver by an event. Now if confusion exists or the mind or the chemistry of the mind is altered by chemical substances like drugs the visualization could be distorted or completely in err. Within the human species and the orders that exist within the human body there are some natural processes in place.

The human body down to the last cell exists through many orders and genetic inheritance. That will conclude for this evening. We will now rest.

Monday, March 22, 1982, Session 142
This is a Wise One.

The soul gives energy to other souls and absorbs energy from other souls. When the soul is with like-souls the energy that is given is received and that which is received is given and energy is multiplied.

This same thought applies to like-thinking. What is verbalized within a group where the group is gathered for a single purpose is subconsciously sending forth electrical-like impulses that permeate the gathering. Humans refer to it as a highly charged atmosphere or gathering. This interchange, whether spoken verbally or mentally, occurs within all dimensions to one degree or another. But the interchange within the Earthly experience is different in the respect that the physical body cannot always avoid internal rejection when not in agreement with the exchange of ideas while the soul body can by projecting itself about what it does not wish to hear, so to speak.

Within the human species those verbal and thoughts are spoken, continually send forth energy. The whole Earth is energized. And mankind can feel the pull of the energy. But those souls on Earth have chosen to experience on Earth and are not meant to run from the earthly experience but are meant to understand the challenge of learning and expressing God's infinite truth. That concludes for this evening.

❀ SOUL AND CHOICE

Monday, November 16, 1981, Session 49 – Excerpt
This is a Wise One.

Choice is the soul living its evolutionary existence. The choice is made every second, every microsecond of a soul's existence. The choice is which alternative to choose in a given experience, situation, emotional response. One may choose an alternative that helps the soul gain greater understanding of all that is and the soul's responsibility to all. This would be a positive choice. A choice might be merely to fulfill the ego of the soul, to fulfill within and not to come from within and expand to without and all that is. These choices occur microsecondly. These choices are the souls, are your choices, as part of free will.

In the earthly experiential cycle, choices are good and positive and not so good and negative, each contribution toward a direction of the soul. Each choice returns to the soul. If the choice is just and positive it returns manifold for man and soul, are from love and essentially good. If a choice is negative it too returns to haunt or to debt the soul *(accumulated as the karma we must then experience and learn from)*. These debts must be recognized and dealt with for the further understanding and development of the soul.

A choice or choices made with love and fairness intended is returned only positively. A choice of deceit is a debt that will be recognized in a soul.

Now a soul has this balance of positive and negative as energy, has a balance of positive and negative, and that is the theory behind energy; and there lies the relationship between soul, thought, and physical substance of the soul and all that is.

If a soul proceeds on a path of negativeness and reinforces that with similar decisions and actions, it will become weighted with a negative charge. It needs a balance. It needs a positive outlook and charge to gain greater energy. No soul will perish for all is a part of God and God is a part of all.

However, a soul that continues upon a primary negative path will continue to accumulate negative energy and that will turn within and slowly, slowly, evolve to a minor, minor, minor, energy that cannot function very well. A soul that accumulates positive energy, positive thought, ever battling in the quest of understanding goodness and of love, will gain much expansive energy illumination and finally a place with evolved souls and a place of creating as a part of God.

This then is what the soul may evolve to. The one clause of fulfillment for a soul is love. Not love for self but love for all. And there, leaps and bounds illuminating energy surrounds the soul as does love.

So, it is a Law of God that the justice in your heart shall be yours. In other words, what you give out, you receive back. When you give out of love from the heart, so shall you receive love.

SOUL WALK-INS *(Exchange Places)*

Wednesday, February 24, 1982, Session 123
This is your Wise Guide.

When the soul is a wise soul having learned that it is made up of many self-evolving free will personalities, it may not enter Earth's experience in quite the same manner. It may choose to exchange places with a soul personality that is currently in experience.

This is done over a period of months for the shock to the physical body and the shock to the casual body would and has caused a violent change in personality, a misfocus, a terrible confusion, about the personality. However, when the change is made there is complete adjustment and the soul dropping in or walking in goes about fulfilling the personality's life objectives and a broader objective.

Now there are other circumstances where the soul walking in may wish to fulfill a debt. Any soul whether incarnating through the birth pattern or through dropping in assumes all the commitments and responsibilities of the functioning personality. Now, memory within the human does not truly exist, at least within the physical body. The memory that a soul on Earth has is memories of past lives which would be soul memories and memory of the current life experience. Now the memory that a walk-in develops loses the same emotional significance and meaning but is more in line with the memory.

For the walk-in, of course, has not lived the experience in order to feed the pain or joy of the memory. Walk-ins prepare and study before walking in. Many walk-ins become famous individuals or well-known individuals, great inventors, artists, mathematicians, etc.

The relation between personality and the physical body amounts to thought processes of the personality and how those processes stimulate or depress various organs and glandular systems with electrical patterns that can be positive or negative.

Sunday, May 23, 1982, Session 174
This is your Wise Guide.

When the soul is evolving and is beginning to understand and apply the soul, need not incarnate from birth forward but may exchange places at a given time or for a given purpose with another soul. Now, this can take a period of time to accomplish for the personality always remains but there is an exchange of wiser souls in all cases. Even in a negative situation, there can be an exchange with a soul who is more familiar with the laws of physics and thought relating to Earth's sphere.

This exchange is normally for the purpose of the betterment of humanity. Now, this is not always the situation for some like yourself, who choose to be born and experience the evolving of a personality and its process of identifying with the greater self and adjusting to the human evolutionary cycle or mankind's current structures.

Incidentally, these structures are basically not different than any structures at any time within Earth's history. There are cycles of evolvement within mankind also and they relate to the human endeavor whether the society is technically advanced or technically regressed, the challenge and the human endeavor is the same.

There are richer and poorer, workers and nonworkers, givers and takers, or many souls incarnate upon Earth through free will and thought. And many souls incarnate together for like purposes or just endeavors. Now a soul exchanging with another soul may do so, also, in certain circumstances to reap just consequences or to save another soul or personality from reaping unjust consequences.

There is within societies, natures, humans, and those justly evolving within the Earth's sphere an ebb and a flow to life. That can best be described by the nature of a pendulum and how it swings. Now those on a path nearest truth can be exemplified by the pendulum standing still and hanging straight or swinging back and forth so rapidly it appears to be calm.

This particular analogy has application in many concepts and realities within the human mind and the emotional mind. However, it is not an all-encompassing analogy upon the emotions of the human mind. But there can be some observations made relative to this principle once one understands and correlates the aspects of negative and positive exchange and neutral application.

The evolving personality being observed can only be measured upon action, reaction, and what that personality openly requires and asks for. And the unique thing about observation is that each looks out and observes relative to what each individual understands and has experienced.

For eons of time, mankind has approached treating the human and other species based upon observations. There is another level by which one can treat, or for that matter, many other levels depending upon perspective. In all dealings with the human personalities, higher concepts and laws apply whether accepted or rejected by evolving souls. To best guide one's self throughout their human lives, one should do what is in one's heart and there will be just evolutionary wisdoms resulting.

When one looks for their answers from mankind one shall receive their answers from mankind. When one looks for their answers from God, one shall receive their answers from God. God is always reconciled and found from within. For even in learning from great Masters, one has to apply from within as best as possible. Mankind is not evil. Mankind each and all have the power of thought by which to create magnificent destinies.

That is all for this evening.

❀ EVOLVING TO UNDERSTAND

Wednesday, August 4, 1982, Session 214
This is a Wise One.

The soul projects various thoughts that travel at various vibrational levels. The soul receives various thoughts projected from those levels that the soul is in tune with. Groups of souls or frames of souls incarnate together to create experiences and play experience roles to come to understand truth.

The soul is the thinker that creates the personality. The personality creates limitations in the human world. The soul removes the limitations of the human world.

When the soul is evolving to understand, the soul predicts that which it plans. The soul predicts through imagery and projection. And that projection will occur. The body houses the soul about it and not within it. The personality emanates from the body. The body seeks to be serving one master or another. The body can serve many masters and will become attached to many different masters. The body can serve the mind, the greater self, God. The body can serve stress, drugs, and other alternatives. The body has been created to serve.

We will conclude for this evening.

Tuesday, June 8, 1982, Session 183
This is a Wise One.

The soul will have a wise evolution when it pursues the path of inner seeking. The human will have a wise evolution within the framework of one's life when it pursues inner understanding of the soul.

When the personality begins to look within and to measure inward growth against outward responses there is a conflict that creates turmoil within and apparent turmoil without. As the personality manifest and apparent revolt against its acceptance standard be it parent, political, or be it sex. The personality is always freely evolving and yet will eventually find its greater self and come to an understanding of whom and what it is.

So, it is with the soul that portions of the soul after collecting the fragments that were manifested in and through experience and coming to a mutual recognition will through order ascend to a God-like state relative to the human endeavor. This is done through all orders so there are tree-Gods, plant-Gods, animal-Gods, earth-Gods, but eventually, orders discover or souls within the orders discover still a greater self that is inner-related and inner-connected and becomes the whole soul and ascends to a God-like state of creating and guiding worlds.

We will conclude for tonight.

✿ SOUL'S EXPERIENCE ON VARIOUS SYSTEMS

Tuesday, December 15, 1981, Session 73
This is a Wise Wise Wise Wise Wise One.

Thought of love creates energy that is formed from acceleration, velocity, frequency, vibration, and is marked by color. The color of an infant soul, a soul with only knowledge of I Am That I Am is white.

Created souls have free will and all souls have two basic instincts: love and creating. There are an infinite amount of alternative life forms and experiences but when one is first created the first planetary life experience is Earth. The last planetary life experience is Marcella.

A soul will experience life on Earth and in other systems. A soul does not remain stagnant. The levels of attainment are presented for the incarnated souls that need a reference point. In reality, there is no level, just degrees of understanding. A soul can maintain that level with the Creator or may through experiencing, alter the conscious state and this always requires a little more time to find truth.

A soul who no longer enters Earth's experience goes on to other experiences forever. A soul that is so highly evolved that they no longer require a physical experience never, never, dies. A soul always creates.

We will now conclude that dictation and ask for questions.

Mike: I don't have any questions, or I have so many I don't want to start asking them.

You may go then. Go and have a good evening.

Saturday, February 20, 1982

We will now write for the book. When a human being is between incarnations, that personality first learns to find its true nature and its individually known greater self through inner search and wisdom. Now, this may require creation of new experiences, not the physical experience, but those of a different vibratory level with other personality souls that are also seeking. Now the personality itself cannot rush back into incarnation without finding at least a portion of its greater self. Some will attempt to reach physical beings that they know, and this is where your historical "ghosts" and possessions come from.

Now through seeking and learning the experiences that are created for this personality, soul, are fulfilling inner yearnings of this soul. It exists, this soul or portion forever whether it finds its greater self or when it is merely seeking, experiencing, and learning, each experience that a portion of a soul experiences becomes a remembered soul experience of the whole.

Now human philosophies, ideals, beliefs, governments, reflect remembered soul experiences and current personality experiences and soul desires, wishes, fulfillments, etc.

This is a reason why there are always and have been always so many different ideals, structures, beliefs, created within the Earth's environment.

Now some of these experiences do indeed when not on Earth, take place on other planets if that is the desire. It is always on a different vibratory level. It is always inherent when each wishes to express and learn.

It is merely expressing and reflecting projected thought in any experience. The experiences are as real, the so-called physical parts of those experiences, are as real yet exist forever.

The soul seeking and experiencing grows in energy in its own eyes and in the eyes of God when it shares with other portions of itself. The reality of all this experiencing and seeking of all the many forms of expression is that they are all seeking and express-ing love in one form or another. I have spoken, we have spoken, I Am have spoken, all here that represent an understanding of love about the human species, but all species, all elements in one manner or another sense they are part of God and within them is incorporated those basic elements within God's laws of love and free will expression within the defined order whether it be human or plant.

When souls gather and express they are doing so justly, cre-atively, and lovingly in one form or another. Now all or each is a part of all and all is consciousness and God.

Mike is shaking.

I AM THAT I AM. I am with you and will guide you. You may stop writing and ask any question, any question about anything or anyone.

Mike: No questions.

Then I will bid you a good evening and the Wise One here will rest for just a bit longer.

Mike slept a long time after that.

❁ SOUL AND PERSONALITY

Friday, April 2, 1982, Session 149
This is a Wise One.

When the soul is a fragment personality it is created out of love by the highest portion of the evolved soul, highest meaning most highly evolved portion. Now the personality, like all creations of beingness, has forged free will and evolves through that free will. Now if the personality had only free will at its base it would relate entirely to Earthly structures, philosophies, and experiences.

However, there is a soul that is a part and projection of a greater self and is a part and a projection of each soul personality. There is an internal battle between the soul and the personality. The soul can only communicate through thoughts to the person-ality. But the personality through free will has the ability to blot out a greater self.

That is all for tonight.

Saturday, May 22, 1982, Session 173
This is a Wise One.

When the soul is focusing through visualization or imagery within the order of humanity there is purpose, desire, intent that is of concern for the soul. The imagery imagines probable lives and probable challenges, not the specifics. For instance, one might visualize being a singer and achieving certain recognition and visualize certain struggles along the way without identifying specific instances. The soul is connected directly through vibration to the fragment personality and feels every thought, every pain through vibrational and color change.

The expression that the soul aches because of certain things the personality does is true in a sense because the personality though freely evolving can go off in its own direction; even after life on Earth will always be connected to its creator and will one day understand its greater self. For each element, fragment, and entity of God, has greater selves and yet each remain themselves forever and ever. Except for those elements who become buried and forgotten in soul memory not to be awakened again unless the soul through un-Godlike or antilove-like behavior reawakens the sleeping personality.

So, in that sense buried deep within the soul, even the negative personality lives forever but could not re-establish itself for it would need more energy and like-energy and this through enlightenment would not happen, probably.

An example, however, Earthly examples never fully express soul's evolvement, would be a human personality on Earth having, shall we say, an emotion or temper that they are finally able to put to rest. They would not want the temper to reawaken itself if it was of a violent nature for it would only bring about unhealthiness, harm, hurt, decreased energy, among some benefits to anger.

🏵 RESPONSIBILITY

Friday, January 8, 1982, Session 87
This is a Wise One.

We will begin tonight by speaking of responsibility.

A fragment/personality has inherent in its being and its experience that which every other element of all that is has; it has love, thought, truth, and is forged with free will.

The soul should have all that for the greatest Earthly understanding possible and follow God's laws. Out of love each soul/fragment on Earth or in any given experience is forged with free will. Souls are images of God's mental experience. They are and do create auras and create out of thought. Souls create their earthly destiny and experience. All souls do this as an expression of free will.

Understanding that God's greatest gift is thought, love and truth, love, thought and truth, thought and love, love, thought, and truth.

We will conclude this evening's session.

Sunday, February 14, 1982, Session 116
I AM THAT I AM.

When a soul is cast forth from God the soul is a thought of love, truth, free will. The soul will spread itself in all directions within a given experience. The soul after experiencing, learning, and understanding love given, is at one with the creative force. This soul may then experience within other realities, may not experience, but merely guide other realities that are infinite and ever expanding. The Earth is not the first experiment in the seeking of love nor would it be the last. Love and God are infinite. All souls are infinite. Some have a longer path to finally reach the destiny of limitless love.

The soul that gives justly from the heart receives many pleasurable lifetimes. The soul that judges shall be judged. For it is written in God's laws that, that which one thinks is reality and shall be received in return. Now confusion does exist within all souls of Earth in that the understanding of love and its power is not freely expressed.

That is all for this evening.

❀ REINCARNATION AND RESOLVING DEBTS

Monday, March 8, 1982, Session 132
This is a Wise One.

When the soul is with like-souls there is an exchange of learning experiences and reincarnational dramas during initial stages of development. Souls do gather with souls of like-interests, destinies, and experiences. This is not a rule but a trend, like a child on Earth who grows and experiences with certain friends, like that child some souls outgrow or are outgrown by developing souls.

There still may be on occasion interplay for various reasons. Generally speaking souls upon Earth relate dramas and live out experience with many of the same souls. Now on Earth, they do come in contact with other souls but much of that is through passing acquaintance. If one on Earth can relate their life it usually revolves around family members and a few select friends.

Upon occasion, the call for justice or purpose is so strong that an individual will appear to be unpredictable in pursuit and action of something that appears out of the normal behavior pattern of the individual.

This is generally planned before incarnating where a test or experience or drama is enacted that will provide necessary learning for the soul and the personality. The specifics of the experience and the drama are not predetermined, just the general outline. For instance, a soul may choose to resolve a debt and plan to become a baseball player and because of various other reasons be injured and therefore act out that debt as a sports writer, manager, or something relating to baseball. A woman may want to be a writer and circumstances prevent that and she may be a critic, an editor, a journalist, or something else relating to writing. So, in essence, the dramas or plays acted and re-enacted have a pliable outline with no predetermined script. This is one play where the actors through free will and choice create the script. Certain dramas can be played and replayed over many lives until there is a just pattern or development.

Now not all souls are always pursuing resolving 'just' debts, some attempt to ignore them not only creating other debts but in one manner or another generally virtually always receiving what they give from the heart.

Through infinite experience, these stories or dramas can be acted within any experience, not just the Earth experience. Not only do families and small groups tend to experience together but nations, countries, even islands tend to incarnate and experience together. The lessons to be learned and practiced are basic and simple. And yet more evolves around them then one can possibly imagine; thought, love, and free will.

This will conclude tonight's dictation. Have a good evening.

WHEN THERE IS NO LONGER A NEED TO REINCARNATE

Tuesday, March 9, 1982, Session 133
This is a Wise One.

When the soul is developing and evolving toward a fuller understanding of God's infinite love of the thought that guides all and of the free will that is inherent in all, there is a projecting by the soul into each order within an experiential system.

Just as each soul has free will and creates through free will, so too each projection within any order has free will and creates freely. Within each order there exist projections that do indeed have a greater self and do indeed seek to understand their God. When the soul experiences love within any order and all orders and when the soul gives love within any order and all orders and further accepts that all are created equally in the Lord's eyes than the soul will no longer have a need to incarnate on Earth. Within each order there too are greater self and there are Gods in higher states of understanding within that order.

When the soul has love bound within it and all projections of a given soul have the fullest possible understanding of their unique shared and individual realities. When that passes, we can say that the soul has evolved to a higher state and when the soul within all the orders that make up a soul come to that understanding and Earthly life holds no personal draw to that soul, only purpose.

Within each order there exist various projections that make up a portion of the soul created by God.

When Earthly incarnations are no longer necessary there is that recognition within the soul that there is no need for Earthly experiences for the self. That is all for now.

❀ REINCARNATION AND EARTH'S EXPERIENCE

Monday, April 26, 1982, Session 161
This is your Wise Guide.

When the soul is first incarnating on Earth within the order of the personality, the soul brings with it, eternal wisdom and understands that the purpose for incarnating on Earth is to practice eternal truths and not just know but understand these truths. Therefore, the soul will, in some manner or fashion, experience the predator and the prey, the lover and the taker, the observer and the fearer. The soul, all souls, must when projecting and creating a personality give and provide free will.

Now each soul understands that its purpose is to find God, greater truths, itself, and reality. Souls evolve not just on Earth but within the sphere of Earths planetary system; (there) are many souls that form and support the solar system.

There is an agreed upon but pliable structure that is a just structure to aide and guide souls in their seeking and practicing of thought, love, and free will.

Now the structures that exist speak of good and evil. And to repeat, there is love, love given, and love held closely that creates justice, that instills order, that is the purpose of free will, that is understanding and evolution.

The "devil" or "Satan' does not exist. Love exists.

The reality of love given is growth in all areas including energy, creativeness, lovingness, thinkingness, love held closely expresses fear, binding, dissipation, containment, and an ever-dwindling energy field. So much so that it can ground souls to Earth.

When one or many of a highly evolved nature bring forth truth upon Earth, by its very nature, it will cause chaos. For Earth is a learning ground, a battleground, a struggle for understanding.

When souls become highly evolved, they at times have a very difficult time focusing within Earthly pursuits. However, the same laws of truth apply eternally forever, infinitely, love all. A love given is a love received, a love held closely is a love held closely, when one gives justice from the heart, one should love that justice for that justice they shall have. God forsakes no one. Some though forsake God.

That will conclude for tonight.

SOUL AND FREE WILL

Monday, March 15, 1982, Session 137
This is a Wise One.

Free will is part of every soul. Free will exists within each soul as an inherent reality. There is no soul that does not have free will. When souls create or project portions of themselves, it is necessary that those portions be forged with free will within a given order. All fragments of a soul have free will. However, human beings do not recognize that in other species and beings.

All fragments of soul have guides that choose that form of expression to evolve. Guides are highly trained, for many of them have not experienced Earth and they must be trained to allow for free will expression within their protégés, so to speak.

Free will is with all souls but one of the tenants of free will is that one soul, or any being possessing free will should not and, in eternal truth, cannot order another's free will. Free will is like love and thought, a natural need, desire, reality, and truth within souls and projected fragments of souls. Free will allows for understanding, creativity, fun, happiness, justice. Free will allows for all, for without free will then would not souls be merely puppets to dance to the tune of their creator and never in themselves create love or think? For without free will they could never have the original desire to express, for their thought would come from a creator and not from themselves. So, all beings and created beings must have, must have free will.

That will conclude for this evening. We will add more information now.

Though free will is inherent within each, it cannot function within a shared reality without love and the laws of love or rather truths of love. Nor can love exist without free will nor can thought exist without free will or free will without thought. Thought is the creator. Free will is the expression. Love is the order. Now we have concluded.

Tuesday, March 16, 1982, Session 138
This is a Wise One.

When the soul is created, throughout the thought of love, the forging of free will is like love and thought inherent in the process for all are born into existence with free will.

Now free will is available and encouraged and yet souls and man through inactivity or nonuse or expression limit their free will expression. When this occurs, fear enlarges and becomes a force of apathy and oppression and hopelessness and yet free will is only large in the eyes of the perceiver.

Many can be led by allowing themselves to be led through a lack of expression of free will. Like all experience in an evolutionary process, patterns of behavior are created whether it be with the soul or the human. To change negative patterns, fear must be faced down.

Even when fear is basically eliminated one still has to function through justice. The wise ones who have gained an understanding of the use of free will also understand that one or more cannot intentionally change another's free will.

Of course, on Earth, this is done within all structures often. One reason for this is because mankind for some time now has not understood the process of thought, love, and free will. When mankind begins to understand that process, there will be changes within structures, beliefs, philosophies, that will bring about and is bringing about chaos. Free will has with love and with thought brought about the creation of beings.

❀ GOD-SOUL

Wednesday, March 24, 1982, Session 143
This is a Wise One.

When the soul is in the God state it creates within the laws of God or creation. The soul even then is evolving to a clearer functioning of love given. It creates and functions within a myriad of experiences always contributing to the fulfillment of all souls. For when one gives one receives manifold.

The God-soul is a part of each projection or each soul. Each soul is a fragment of the source or creator. There are three orders that form the whole or truth: thought, love, and free will. Thought creates, free will expresses, love functions and guides.

Within the God-soul various portions are projected into dimensions of evolving souls. Those portions go by the name of Gods or Wise Ones. They are the teachers of evolution. They are the truth bearers that speak truths only so far as they can be accepted by seeking souls. Each religion and philosophy refer to these souls in various fashions. Mythological God, angels, wise ones, teachers, priests, they are in fact teachers and guides. But we only speak of the human personality evolutionary process for there are many other orders in the evolution of the soul and they too have Gods, wise ones, and other names attributing to them, but truth permeates all elements.

God-souls create and are whole worlds. They move about freely. When the soul reaches the state of co-creating there is an initiation rite by which the soul teaches. The soul newly created evolves to understand what it inherently knows, that thought creates the soul and the infinite supreme thought is love given and through love given free will manifests itself for that is the only way that love can grow. That will conclude tonight's session.

HOW SOUL DREAMS

Notebook #34, Page 7
They are ready.

If a man were to take a trip and begin at 8 A.M. and made a destination at 8 P.M., in earth hours he would have traveled twelve hours. If a man were to dream during that trip, he would dream maybe a whole life. It is possible in the mind.

Now when the man had arrived at 8 P.M., he would have lived a whole life in that dream.

Now in a sense the soul dreams; it dreams through visualization and thought projection, the visualization is experience. The soul can project into many experiences at once. The thought projections are focused into various realities and experiences and through order experience. Each projection is, by infinite truth and universal law forged out of thought, as has just been said, love and free will.

Truth, thought, love, and free will exist in each projection. Each projection functions within the framework of order as a projection of love, thought, and free will. All exist in truth expressed freely to degree, (understanding), the soul exists forever in infinite truth and functions for and by infinite truth. That is the only time for the soul.

Man exists in experience as a soul projection defined in time by the experience and order. That is all for tonight.

✿ LOST SOULS

Sunday, April 4, 1982, Session 150
This is a Wise One.

The nature of evil is self-love. Now a soul that is at the depths of depredation is marked by the color black. Interpretations from ancient, ancient writings in the past have taken that blackness and ascribed to black skinned humans negatively and enslaved them.

There is absolutely no connection between skin color and soul color, absolutely no connection. Skin color is a throwback to locality of human beings and a necessity to adapt to certain weather types. Now the soul marked by the color black is a rare, rare, lost soul. It is not your Hitlers, it is past that stage. It cannot without help manifest enough energy to focus within Earthly reality as anything more than an insect or smaller animal. Now they do have the opportunity to incarnate as humans for God forsakes no one. However, it is many Earthly years between incarnations and much care in guidance is taken to the placement of such a personality for they are greatly helped by others for they lack the energy to fully manifest themselves into a human personality.

Color and denseness go hand and hand; they are lost, lost souls who have refused help. But all souls will find their way back to the Creator through infinity, through order, through justice. For all souls are forged with free will and are thoughts of love. There are other realities in which these souls can work their way through that are not of the Earth. However, they will spend eons of time on Earth justly so. There are souls on Earth today that are just such souls.

Nor should one go out of their way to destroy a pest if the pest would not cause harm. On another order, and we identify no pests as such a vehicle, for even good loving love given souls send forth or have sent forth or will send forth a minute fragment to experience all realms.

This is not in every case but is in a few cases. Evil is defined by mankind that these souls within soul reality and not experiential reality cannot harm evolved souls. They cannot, specifically speaking, stand in the light of such a soul. They are chained unto themselves bound by fear, doubt, insecurity, terror, anguish, and just as it is not possible to describe the beauty of highly evolved, highly evolved souls, so too, a full unhappy description cannot be brought forth to describe the state of these souls. There are so many multidimensional aspects of that state to defy description. Simply said, within evolvement of the soul to God in its supreme form there are many paths, all paths leading back to the source that never dies.

And, so too, one path to describe it as one is not unfortunate, what is thought of as a positive direction. And it ascribes to the power of thought without understanding that love and free will are part of a trilogy of supreme truth. So, it can come to realize the power of thought, even misused, and there are such souls that populate the Earth and given conditions within humanities, development in a particular time in history these souls fight among themselves as well as all.

Now we avoid talking much about this unfortunate reality for our purpose is to give love to all, All. But upon Earth now there are such souls. They consider this a unique time in Earth's history and wish to assume control of mankind for personal gain. Their opportunity to do such is at a time when there are enough souls living in fear and doubt, enough personalities not looking within, not looking without for answers upon Earth that can and will be led. And it appears unfair and unjust when they are about, for the truly highly evolved soul cannot assert force upon free will without breaking a universal law of evolvement.

✽ EVOLUTION OF A SOUL

Thursday, May 13, 1982, Session 169

I Am that I Am. I am with you, I am in you. Within the evolution of a soul, there are cycles, there are experiences that are multidimensional and are created by thought within the shared reality of all evolving souls. Each reflection or creation of a soul by law is infinite in nature. Now evolving souls experience through the soul's mind and create many experiences at once. In the soul's mind, there are many realities that are experienced. There are other realities other than Earth, other than Earth's solar system. Infinity is forever.

The evolution of the soul is forever and ever and ever. There are souls that spend eons of time evolving through experience to understand truth. There are souls locked into mistaken realities that are what Earth refers to as lost. There are an infinite number of philosophies, structures that extend far beyond Earth's order. Some personalities and soul reflections get lost for eons of time looking and following paths that they themselves create in a search for peace.

All souls when first created go forth and experience to understand what they know. The evolution of Earth within the minds of evolving souls is billions of years old relative to human thinking, billions of years.

Within written and within soul memories are by this that are recalled as civilizations. Atlantis and Lemuria are but two of more civilizations than mankind will ever know.

Some have faint memories and describe cycles of races. Some attribute these races to other planets within your solar system. Some souls have incarnated in more civilizations than others. What is difficult for the human mind to understand is that Earth's solar system and all experience is the dream world of evolving soul that has no time just now. So, humans on Earth are but one line, one evolutionary line of development for the soul, but all times, developments, experiences, and reflections are part of God, for God is All. And none are truly lost for infinity is forever.

I Am That I Am I exists within all souls as a love that no one on Earth can understand, as "thought" that no one on Earth can understand. And all souls are created in my image as I have been created in the image of God, for God is All.

The energy and power of a soul is and can be indescribably powerful. Each element of reality and each element of experience remain as a part of the soul's evolvement forever. Each personality on Earth lives forever, forever in the memory and reality and experience and projection of soulness.

Each line of development or created experience is agreed upon by groups of souls for the purpose of learning truth. The agreement is guided by 'highly' evolved souls whose purpose and function are to contribute and live and support and guidelines of evolutionary experience and development. These souls are the highest God or the God of All for they give to support and aide all. Their soul mind is greater, more magnificent, more grandiose, tremendous, and splendid. An infinite variety of beautiful words could never describe the completeness of these glorious wise infinitely wise loving creating souls.

They communicate within all realms as teachers. They know that to elevate souls and fragments returns to them more energy and they do it in light of giving already knowing eons of time ago that they automatically receive manifold what they give.

So, there is within the truth of soulless the reality of soulness multidimensional growth. And the human and all species and all evolutionary lines and Earth type experience are but one thin line from the perspective of the greater soulness that becomes greater and greater and infinitely greater.

And the beauty is that God is so wonderful that all that is created, is created in this image to become to God and a part of a God.

Each line, evolutionary line of development, goes through cycles of evolvement that are fairly planned by participating souls. The cycles within cycles cannot be comprehensively described for they are freely evolving. As a method of reaching God-like states an infinite number of paths have been created by which to find God.

These paths are described in various ways and within all evolutionary lives of development; after eons of time there reaches a point when the truth, the simplicity of truth, is manifested again within an evolutionary line of development without symbols and yet within the framework of symbol for man, of course, is a symbol as the male, as the female, as the race, color, and creed.

Within the evolutionary development of beingkind, shall we say, the structures and cycles sometimes become lost and the evolutionary line for lack of a better description is put back on track. And some souls leap the gap, cross the bridge, transcend the cycle, into truth. Those souls intrinsically and externally know who they are and of course, are helped by others. No soul is lost to God.

Here are simple words that speak the truth of soulness that directly relate to all and also to beingness on Earth. There is thought, there is freedom of thought, there is creating, there is order, there are justice and love, infinite love that transcends all and is a part of all. Accept what you are and accept what all about you are. Inhibit not another soul's creating and evolving and they shall not inhibit yours, indeed you do receive what is given; that is the justness of God. Those who do not yet understand the laws have the simplicity of love truly lie in two simple statements that mean so much. "A love given is a love received. A love held closely is a love held closely."

There are many probable and possible occurrences that indeed form their own cycle and find their way back to the truth of love. Those will be explored in the course of your lifetime and even after your lifetime.

Each reader and seeker should understand if they choose to, that love does exist within all. And truly all have been created equally in God's eyes. All evolutionary developments are ordered and set so that each order is intricately linked and by nature and by survival must contribute to the other order even down to the basic everyday living.

All reality truly is a shared reality. It is not expected within humankind that comprehension of all orders be there, else why would they be incarnating as humans. It is just simply stated without judgment, to simplify living, for this is done with love and understanding on the part of highly evolved souls. There are certain responsibilities that we would ask of humankind and within all other orders of development.

We shall indeed ask this of humankind but not this evening. For you, just live your life and do what is in your heart, intent is what matters. We add one more thing. There will always be structures and philosophies by which mankind and soul-kind within any evolutionary line will follow. But the laws simply and justly stated transcend all existence. And each freely evolutionary element will indeed follow some line of development in their search for truth justly so. And in your everyday living, there are indeed just consequences and returns for that which you intend and that which you do. Intent reaps the greater by far.

That will conclude for this evening's writing.

Tuesday, August 3, 1982, Session 213

This is a Wise One.

The soul evolves through degrees of understanding. The soul is focused in all realities from the greatest stars to the dust of the Earth. Now, this is accomplished through a relationship with other souls within other orders. The orders make up all of the experience within an evolutionary cycle.

Now the soul as a total soul itself evolves through each system of reality until it has spent some time within each reality. It is then at one with creators, the God of Gods, the supreme of supremes. The soul will follow the cycles of a given reality until it has evolved through that reality. It will begin again and again to re-experience certain experiences until it understands and is ready to move on to other experiences.

The soul evolves to understand love and law. Law being defined as a reality of love. When the soul has evolved and understands by being a player in a large play and a practicing creator it evolves and sometimes to be a practicing God. Now use the term practicing God to explain why the different God concepts occur. Gods evolve within a God-world, as souls evolve in a soul world, as mankind or any order evolves in a matter or material type of world.

Truth exists in all worlds. The soul that becomes a larger creator is part of a group of souls. The soul then in a greater sense is always a practicing creator at one level or one degree of understanding or another.

The soul experiences each order within the reality of that order to support the experience. Within an experience then each is truly connected, however, uniquely individual in an ordered manner. Each creation of the soul then lives on forever and yet when the soul evolves out of one reality to another it takes with it memories of the experience.

The life itself or experience itself provides the soul the experience to gain further learning and understanding. The soul knows no pain than that which it creates for itself. When the soul reaches a level of awareness, it comes to understand that it is no more or no less than God or any element of God.

The soul can only take with it what it was given upon creation: love, peace, creating. It focuses within all realities and when it understands its nature, it is at peace and works to help all other parts of itself for it is no greater or less than any other part.

The soul thinks and is thought forever. The soul freely thinks and within any reality comes to understand that freedom without law and discipline will work or possibly will destroy. The perceived self, the ultimate objective is happiness. One learns to give up what hampers one's happiness. Each is at a different level of understanding regarding that. There comes a time when the soul reaches a point of development where the soul accepts certain realities expecting nothing to keep for the self and giving only what it needs for peace and happiness.

We speak not of material giving, we speak of the giving from within. Do what feels peaceful and happy and right and you will be doing what God intended. All will reach God in one manner or another. There are many a number of paths and yet where it is, is now. God can be reached now, the channels are there, the frequencies are there, and the truth is there. And each touch upon that truth in their life fleetingly, but each does.

That truth of giving love and absolutely expecting nothing but realizing true love that one will receive when one gives. By treating others as you wish to be treated so you shall evolve, so you shall be judged, not by others, by your own intentions and thoughts.

That concludes tonight's session.

We wish to make a comment as an aside regarding the senses of the human. The human senses can attune itself to various vibrational levels and pick up through reflected vibrational levels certain sounds, smells, and visions, etc. Certain feelings, it is a very functional system that has evolved in time. That is all.

✿ SOUL SCHOOL

Wednesday, August 11, 1982, Session 217
This is a Wise One.

When the soul is focused within the experience known as Mandanar *(Written as it sounded.)* the soul is on a path, one of many of lights. Mandanar is a school located in the realm of Nebulon *(Written as it sounded.)* the 3rd Universe of Nebulon, one of the many spellings to pronounce the same word.

This is a school where one understands poverty, anguish, and death. Now this could have many names for there are many schools in the evolutionary process. Mandanar is a school where one talks about an upcoming incarnation and plans for the birth and circumstance. Now each is born into or focuses into Earth and themselves and a freely evolving soul into physical reality. Now there are many schools and there are many paths that train and prepare one's entry into a physical or vibrational experience.

It is done to set the stage for just happenings *(i.e. resolving debt)*. Now the free will personality in one way or another will have those circumstances occur in one manner, or one timeframe or another.

✿ SOUL AND ORDERS OF BODY

Wednesday, November 17, 1982, Session 273
When a soul is focused within the human body it is part of a body made up of many orders. The soul adopts that body as an image, as does the personality adopt strongly that image. Now the personality contains within it an emotional body or aura and a newly developed mind-body. This mind-body can be potentially just what is learned within the current human endeavor. However, when this body is outside of the physical body it can accumulate more kindness. It can build thoughts and a life for itself to a limited degree. The body may continue for a period of experience

after the physical body has died accumulating more experience but as a singular personality it cannot reincarnate, cannot create other bodies.

When the personality is reunited with portions of its greater self, it takes with it the body of knowledge, learned, but loses its emotions. This is done in varying degrees depending upon the understanding of the soul or personality. It is much easier to give up the emotions when not focused on the physical body for there is no feeling to go along with the emotions. This personality though can create and travel various places within its vibrational capability. It can travel any place on the Earth that it chooses.

Normally this does not occur for it becomes quickly evident to this personality mind that no matter how hard it tries it cannot become part of the physical world any longer. There are, however, other vibrational worlds that it can become a part of. It chooses those worlds. For instance, one may have a need or desire to play a sport or a game and center themselves around that endeavor. Eventually, though it finds its way back to its true self and discovers that it is the dream and not the reality, that it is a part of something greater.

All personalities that leave the human body can find like personalities and may find and almost always do find, for a period of time, friends and relatives to greet them.

The personality emotion body will spend time learning at the correct vibrational level. It will stay there as long as it wishes and will be granted any wish that its mind requests. But like Earthly humans, this personality will have to receive the wish in a manner that can be understood.

THOUGHT

Thought is all, creates all;
reflected thought experiences the
evolutionary path of love given.

Thought is a part of all consciousness,
even atoms and molecules are thought created.

CHAPTER 4

THOUGHT

Imagine walking into a room with one or more people and immediately feeling good, or uneasy. What you are feeling is the thought put forth by others; thoughts create energy; all of our experience is created through thought. Within the following sessions, the souls speak of the power of thought in the creation of soul and one's reality, and how each thought carries its own vitality and reality and is the driving force behind all creation.

So, come sit with us.
These messages are meant for you.

(DICTATION BEGINS)

❁ WHAT THOUGHT IS

Sunday, January 16, 1982, Session 94

I am a Wise, Wise, Wise One.

Thought is more than you know. Thought indeed is all that you know. All is created through thought. Thought has more significance even in Earthly life than is known to mankind. Thought is created, even on Earth, and capable of moving objects. Thought is a part of all consciousness, even atoms and molecules are thought created. Thought is within each element of God, within each order of God. Thought creates all experience. There are thought patterns that are not like yours but are nevertheless even found in molecules.

There is not a random combination that creates what you know and do not know, it is through thought. Each molecule is indeed forged with free will but not the same free will within your order.

The Supreme One who has created all includes each element of all and all is God.

When a soul—as you recognize soul—is understanding of love, the soul then becomes a co-creator of whichever experience the soul is involved in. Now in a sense, all elements and souls are co-creators for that which we think indeed is what we create.

However, I am speaking on a more practical, so to speak, level. Thought will form seen and unseen manner, thought will create anything that one wishes. Now to create free will, molecules, cells, atoms, souls, requires giving and knowledge of basic principles that can only be found through love. To create for others indeed creates for oneself. To create for the self diminishes the power to create at all for the particular creator.

Thought is projected through frequency and through a co-operative effort between elements of orders within orders. *(See a definition for "order" at the end of this book.)* If an evolved soul wishes to project upon Earth or any soul for that matter and wishes to become a part of Earth's experience, it requires the cooperation of other souls, of course, but the Earth itself, the human bodies and orders within orders . . . within orders.

For the physical order of Earth is not the same as the order of soul. That which is created on Earth has been created by many, All That Is and I Am that I Am. It began with a general idea of experience and what form would be taken. Experiments were done, and man was created, not evolved from something, but created through a cooperative effort between molecules, atoms, etc. that made up Earth's elements and experience.

Saturday, January 22, 1982, Session 99
Hippocrates worked on the principle of thought and was instrumental in setting up new medical procedures. Hippocrates felt that through the nervous system and nerve endings one could revitalize the body. When he did experiments, they were successful in many cases.

Now in all life, in all elements, there are so-called nerve endings in which the electrical impulses of thought work. There are unknown frequencies in emitting thought.

Now all experience is created through thought. All that you know on Earth is thought. You are thought, the human being part. When thought creates anything, frequency from acceleration and velocity is involved thereby creating various forms of energy or life. When one individual personality wishes to communicate with any other element, it can be done through thought and the thoughts that are thought are picked up by all, about you.

Write this: Thought is the projection of imagery. Thought is reflected energy, perception is reflected thought. What one sees is a reflection of a projection.

That is all for this evening.

Monday, February 8, 1982, Session 111
This is a Wise One.

Thought is formless consciousness that assumes form through visualization. Thought is linked to like-thought within a shared reality. Thought through shared reality creates the soul's experiential endeavor. Thought is love for creating, can only be accomplished through love given. This is a universal infinite law of creation, reality, experience, evolution, infinity, truth, God, when thought is confined to love withheld it lacks free will, creative ability, and infinite life.

If a thought is created for love's internal seeking as opposed to love's external truth, then oblivion is the destiny of that thought. There is a paradox then. Both are thoughts of love, both are seeking infinite truth. Love given is upon the righteous Earth. Love turned towards the self is and must be extinguished to start treading the righteous path. For what is the gain of thought of only the self? It is not even fun; it requires much work against one's self, for the nature of all, is "love given."

Now when an order is created, there are perimeters by which an element of the soul exists within that order. There are many orders that are contained within a single soul that when expressing in Earth's solar system, all orders are contained within a single soul.

The human order is but one. Souls are created and yet create. Within Earth's experiential solar system all that each order sees, senses, and experiences are reflected thought.

Within the order of Earth's solar system from consciousness observation, all is projected thought. Sustained and created with love, free will, and destiny, to find infinite love and God.

The God that is ever expanding, ever creating. The God of love given, that transcends all.

Thought is all, creates all. Reflected thought experiences an evolutionary path of love given. What assures each element of God's infinite love given, is the law of justice. Justice is love given and justice is a part of the paradox of love given and love turned toward the perceived self.

For that which thought creates returns in creating, through love given, the return is manifold. For it is ever expanding when applied to love of perceived self; the return is of the self and is ever contracting for self-love, is eventual oblivion.

All consciousness, all consciousness experiences at a given time self-love, for to understand love given, one must experience contrasting love. There is no predetermined time that determines when the soul is reunited with that creative force of truth, that creative force that permeates all. That infinite thought of love which is the only truth.

It, that final wisdom, comes at a different time for all elements of God, but it comes to all. For even the most selfish come to realize the path of oblivion and relinquishes the self and begins to freely give love, but justice must be fulfilled. For that which was done for the self must be undone.

Bless all with love, have a lovely evening.

Notebook #35, Page 20
Thought is the driving force behind energy. Thought is beingness. Souls, when between incarnations or as developing elements within an order, all have thought freely initiating their own particular evolution.

Now all personalities go on to learn infinitely with other like souls. These other like souls are from the same creator and form the shared reality of existence.

That one has many lives is true. That a soul works out these lives through experience is not true. The personality is not the soul, it is a thought projection of the soul. The personalities form the elements of the total soul just as the souls form the elements of the total God.

Thought created the soul, infinitely living within God's organization. The personality infinitely lives within the soul's organization.

THE WAY THOUGHT WORKS

Sunday, January 10, 1982, Session 88
This is a Wise One.

The way that thought works in the personality everyday life is much the same way that thought works with the soul and is similar to the way that thought works with other dimensions, other experiences, other orders, and is similar to the way that thought works for all that is, and all that is, is Love and God.

Now it is simple and yet can be difficult to fathom love's purpose and reality. In one's everyday life, in the personality, in this time in Earth's history and that occasional time in Earth's history, there comes a buildup of fears and earthly pursuits that trap the personality's thought processes when the personality looks for answers from mankind and from what mankind has created, as opposed to what creative thought has created *(looking within for answers)*.

Now one can point and discuss what does not seem to be right or even understood. In so doing, one can find the answer, but it is much easier to seek to understand what precisely the thought of love creates.

One example that can touch upon each personality now reading these words is to stop and think about the times when out of an act of love for no other reason other than you wanted to, you gave something good of yourself expecting nothing in return. That something might be a word of encouragement to a fellow personality. When doing this you immediately felt exhilarated, charged with more energy than usual, maybe even light-headed, for it made you feel for that moment fulfilled, happy, energetic. And anyone reading these words has felt that. The mother, the father, the child, have felt that.

Now imagine that feeling of happiness, you can expand that just by putting into practice thoughts of love and your life will begin to change. Love is so powerful that even the one may not understand this truth for it truly is the basis of being. One may still advance by practicing love. There are infinite examples of how love given is love received. Each reader can relate to a time when through giving they received.

All of the personality's life on Earth and within the soul element after Earth is seeking and understanding the nature of itself, and that nature is love. For those seeking love and understanding outside of themselves you have admired great artists, the greatest created out of love, you have admired great writers, the greatest created out of love, you have admired great musicians, performers, leaders. The ones you remember, created out of love; what you remember was done out of love. The songs, the poems, the talks, the thoughts. All that you live is reflections of love. Talked about, thought about, accepted, denied, philosophized, discussed, the whole of our purpose and our actions of your thoughtful lives has been understanding love and will always be understanding love.

When it is understood whether by personality, soul, or any element of God's infinity that love is the thought by which you create or by which you respond in some manner. The more one seeks love, the more one grows to understand the supreme wisdom, infinite wisdom of love. The whole of nature from the tiny atom and portions of atoms to elements that you do not know or see, all is out of love and love is a part of all.

Sunday, January 3, 1982, Session 83
This is a Wise Wise Wise One.

In truth one might say that life and a body in which you live is really the dream state for everything that happens—happens through thought.

In total consciousness, each thought including the smallest daydream, or random thought, exists and is a free will thought standing as energy to be picked up and heard by other souls.

Now when one is in the human form, or for that matter, if one is in one natural form the only thoughts that will register as reality are thoughts of intent directed at the personality or soul or random thoughts.

Now the energy that thought has is essentially what one would call noncharged; to convert to a positive or negative, it must find a receiver or another soul. At which time the other soul accepts, allows the thought to pass, or repels the thought. Now a thought, like a human body, has a life span and depending upon the validity and acceptance of the thought, can last for eons of time or a few seconds. Words are not necessarily thoughts so what one speaks is not necessarily what we are referring to. Now the thought of a personality has validity and a life, also. Now it could be, and in a sense, it always is the thought of the greater self, interpreted or filtered by the personality.

Many thoughts are picked up in the dream state. Now a negative thought purposely directed at an enlightened or positive individual, be it personality or soul, will be repelled or passed through. This is a situation where like attracts like, opposites do not attract.

Now in relating this to the personalities, to each individual on Earth, each has experienced walking into a room with one or more people and immediately feeling good or what you call high, or feeling depressed, or what you call bad or merely uneasy. This is the thought shared reality around you.

In a family, a child, a spouse, relative, many times will pick up thoughts being positive or negative. And depending upon the inner understanding of the individual may respond to those thoughts or try and repel those thoughts be a positive or negative, or be the individual positive or negative.

In ancient times, mankind understood and could use the power of thought to move large objects, to heal, to create and to exist. Now as much positive or negative as thoughts create a singular personality or individual, turning those thoughts inward or holding those thoughts within can create a state of depression or elation.

For those thoughts to magnify within the individual they must be cast forth, which also explains the nature of how justice works and why souls do indeed on their own volition wish to pay debts. Not only is it justice and just, but it is also necessary to the substance of the soul. It indeed is a law of God that the justice in your heart you shall have. Again, let us say that words are not necessarily the thoughts that we speak of, some people just seem to talk to be talking. Thoughts of purpose and intent are the thoughts that do the greatest benefit or harm to the soul.

Now in your culture and other cultures on our planet this concept could be valuable and given the greater member of structure of fear and guilt that your establishment has, could cause a great deal of stress within the individual.

Let it be understood that each thought of purpose and intent is indeed a thought of life and creativity be it positive or negative. Your whole world and all existence indeed are based upon thought. There is not one portion of existence of any kind that is not based upon thought.

Now at this time let us say to each who can hear this thought and we offer it to all—love is the seed and is the supreme thought that is the way.

A love going is a love coming. A love staying is a love staying.

What is good, is good for all. If it is only good for the few or one then it is false. Now thoughts do indeed determine all, and your very physical existence, your experience, your life, your love, your anxieties, and your death, such as it is, for, of course, there is no death. Not all these are conscious thoughts and that is probably very good, for in some instances the greater self must work very hard to communicate with an individual personality who is so ego-centered that they cause greater harm to themselves and the soul. It is a painful experience for the soul, the individual, and all, for each is a part of each and all are a part of each. So, a negative soul that causes wrath, destruction, murder, hurts all, hurts the greater self and the personality and reaps much justice for the misinterpretation of love, for there are false loves as well as truth in love.

Now to give you an idea of some of the magnitude of every plant, vegetation, molecule, animal, in a vicinity of a thinking consciousness, will feel, effect, and understand on a communicative level that humans never experience on Earth. Just as animals, plants and those that we mention do not experience thinking as the human species does on Earth.

Wise One (to my mother): Is your hand tired? Would you like a break?

Kathleen: No.

Now thoughts are also visualizations and may be and are perceived slightly differently by each free will soul. The chair that two people see is not the same, the painting that two people see is not the same, for each peer through, so to speak, their own rose-colored glass. But further understanding the nature of visualism and imagery, a great truth, that many know and not understand is that they have visualized their whole life and do indeed visualize their experiences on Earth. Those that understand this can dream great dreams. Those that dream great dreams can, if chosen, make them a reality.

Now before there was a human body, when souls cast forth a causal body that was transparent and indeed is the body of your personality today. They experienced Earth in those terms and in a simplistic statement after seeing plant life and animal life as a minute nature, they chose the human form as a similar one that you have today, to experience Earth and always to seek justice and a path of righteous love.

A goal in each moment of Earth's life and all consciousness is empathy. The greatest thoughts and the hardest for some to visualize come from within and from the greater self who has a vast range of experience and a greater understanding of any personality bar none. So, in common sense, "down to Earth" terms, do not limit any personality to accept a greater self from within to provide answers, it expands not only the greater self but the personality magnitude what you on Earth has, greatness.

For the wisest words on Earth and the wisest words in total consciousness, the wisest thought on Earth and the wisest thoughts in total consciousness can be spoken by anyone. And they are always thoughts of selfless love, of love given.

That will conclude our conversation and thinking for tonight.

Notebook #37, Page 7
This is a Wise One.

The stories of God and Gods are related through what those humans refer to as fantasy and myth but in reality, have truth and validity to them. Every thought has some sort of truth in that it remains as a part of the entity forever but is buried within the entity to surface in an ordered manner until the refinement of that thought has occurred, even random thoughts which are about the cosmos and are a part of the evolutionary development of the cosmos.

Like-thoughts gather in the form of electrical magnetical attraction and form physical occurrences that are thought of as experience and reality in an ordered manner. The thoughts surface creating positive and negative polarization, which alter the physical appearance but will eventually settle into infinite formless thought of God or all that have evolved through the Earth's solar experience. Now when that is achieved, this infinite solar thought and the conclusion of Earth's solar experience or "thought," then God will, and all will be in peace, love, happiness, and at a period of rest and relaxation until the next experience is formed and ordered and created through and by what those on Earth would refer to as the God soul.

The creative laws of love, justice, and order, will always prevail. There is an evolutionary reality to all thought even the relatively inconsequential thoughts of singular human beings.

Evolution will occur and has occurred within Earth's solar experience through the ordered thoughts of all and there are those "wiser" elements of God at this time creating a change in the evolutionary development of Earth's solar system. This change occurs in an ordered manner and is meant to be so.

Creating through an evolutionary experience then will always run a course of conclusion that will come to be understood as love through evolution.

✿ CREATIVE EFFORT THROUGH THOUGHT

Wednesday, January 6, 1982, Session 86
We will now discuss the creative effort through thought.

Thought is all and will create whatever one wishes to create. Thought has, of course, created the soul and the soul, of course, has created the fragment.

The fragment focused in humanness, or physical reality, on Earth begins to create and express from within the fragment. (See the definition for "fragment" at the end of this book.) Now thought can be suppressed when in physical reality a child becomes focused into the fine limitations and is raised and schooled to accept anything out of those confined limitations as evil, as insane, as antisocial. So, the child creates first within the framework of a child and grows to young adulthood living in a social framework, religious framework, scientific framework, biological framework, psychological frameworks, defined by Earth's structures that are, of course, man-made through thought.

Now within the individual thought can be misdirected or suppressed by fear and rejection. An example would be a man and a woman sitting in a room wanting companionship, wanting to express themselves on a psychological level, maybe even wanting to express themselves on a physical level and they may sit there wrapped up in thoughts which they believe to be fantasy, desires limited by structural beliefs, religious beliefs, social beliefs, scientific beliefs. Each walks out of the room having just said a few words and not the words that were in their heart, feeling a little sorry, a little disappointed, a little angry and disappointed that they did not express their good intentions.

Now mankind goes through life seeking structures, not looking within and accepting natural thoughts, for those this may be termed evil, insane, lustful, or whatever the pervading structure determines.

Logically enough, those that you hold up as great people in the various fields in one way or another grew out of those structures facing themselves, treading new ground—defining new ideals.

The individual sees these other individuals as more intelligent, a better artist, a better athlete, and yet, believe it or not, this does not have to be.

Thoughts to be creative are expressed in some matter or form through love even if it is a misguided love. Thoughts that are guided by fear are reactionary and short-lived for they must constantly change and adjust seeking to redefine new answers. When fear is faced, or love is sought, creativity becomes natural and the balance of nature seems to fit comfortably within the mind of the love thinker. Thoughts are exchanged and are about you every second and moment of your eternal experience, whether on Earth or on true reality, none as consciousness.

Thoughts are not always represented by words for on Earth today what one says is not necessarily what one thinks, which of course greatly limits communication on Earth and causes new barriers to be formed. Because authority says it is bad, no matter what authority, does not necessarily make it bad; it can only be bad if you perceive it to be bad. It can only be a problem if you perceive it to be a problem.

Those on Earth all have hopes, dreams, and wishes, to visualize through thought a probable possibility and to follow through action will simplify and make your lives much happier. When one takes the individual and multiplies by many shared beliefs, they will make shared structures; if enough people think something and will it to make it so, will come about whether on a conscious or subconscious level.

Animals and plants have their own method of so-called thinking and it is not the so-called thinking that you possess.

The order of animal is not what you would think. Communication through heightened senses, plants and alike, are through sound frequencies, color, and be it the human, animal or plant, species respond to love as the supreme thought.

To begin to understand yourself and looking within, or rather, through looking within there is a struggle and a battle, so accept and express one's natural love for all based upon fear, determined by that which man has structured. There is no individual that is different from any other individual, any other form of life on Earth as far as that infinite connection to all life, love is concerned.

One not guided by fear could arrive on your planet not having your education, not having been limited by structural man-made frameworks, and given they could learn the language and apply universal laws of love, could do quite well on Earth. Of course, that new arrival would have an advantage of not having 'being' raised of a structure, of not being spiritually born in a structure. Thought not only creates and fulfills your hopes, dreams, and wishes—we do not speak of fantasies here—but can further create illnesses. Many people rarely get sick just because of their attitude and their thought processes. Others may get sick quite frequently. To be the person one wants to be, the first and final step is love and that understanding love is not just for Sundays or Christmas holidays; love is for all seasons and all times and a part for all around you. If you would know that the amount of love in every atom and molecule as part of consciousness you would be overwhelmed.

We will rest.

This is a Wise One. Thought is transmitted by different levels of communication, different frequencies—so to speak. So many do much of their thinking in the dream state while sleeping and actualize their experience soon after their thought or if it is a thought in the future, somewhere in the future.

Some achieve various hypnotic states and communication with like-souls, with like-development and belief, exchanging ideas and thoughts without verbalizing and fully understand what is occurring. Let it be stressed again that each individual does indeed have the free will to think and behave in any matter that they wish.

Thinking intuitively is natural and allows for your true creative expression. Letting others do your thinking for you is unnatural, and of course, you have many lifetimes in which to learn that in all its various ramifications.

Now, there are theories that men and women think differently, but that is not true; no soul on Earth thinks any differently than any other soul. They merely respond differently to thought processes, three-dimensional concepts and their understanding of truth, infinite truth.

Now mankind and the individual soul have spent eons of time living the Earth experience and creating all situations that occur on Earth through thought. To wish something not there because it is negative will not make it go away. To think something not there and to face it down will make it go away. Each on Earth understands that and each person can relate specific experiences of facing down and facing fear, for fear and doubt are no longer there on that particular situation.

Love's justice will prevail, and it is not justice or judgmental conditions placed on the individual by others, by God, by signs, but the justice within each determines the desiring of each, the pursuit and path of each, and each is a part of the whole and cannot be separated, and each has a part of the whole within them. So, the nature of this shared reality is such that giving justly to all that thought of love elevates all. The supreme power understanding on Earth exists within the smallest element of life. When that element or individual comes to that realization, that love is truth and cannot be denied.

End of dictation.

Are there any questions?

Mike: No.

Then have a good evening.

This is your Wise Guide. If there are questions of any nature you may ask them now.

Mike: What happens to the organs and tissues when a body dies? The skeleton remains; does it disintegrate?

It decomposes and gives nourishment to the earth. Each contributes to each. That is the order of truth and, in fact, of life on Earth. Through free will within the human species, the manner in which contributions can be made is by choice. Are there more questions?

Mike: I have no more questions. Kathleen: I have no questions.

Then you may go.

This is Gandhi. To do nothing is almost impossible to improve upon. To do something whether a right or wrong can be improved upon.

PERSONALITY AND THOUGHT

Saturday, January 30, 1982, Session 104, Page 1
This is a Wise One.

Dreams and imagery are thought and are the only reality. Each species, order, personality, and planet, is a thought projection.

All consciousness contributes to any experience, and any experience is thought. On Earth, everything is a thought projection and each order element is and perceived through reflected thought. The whole of consciousness is all that is. And the whole of consciousness creates all experiencing, the Earth and its solar system is just one of many.

Now a thought is forever where there is intent. Like-thoughts attract. Positive loving thoughts grow, and a love given grows and returns. Negative unloving thoughts are attracted to depressed nonunderstanding elements of God and deprive those elements of their God-given love, understanding, free will, and energy. This law applies in the Earth's experience as well as it does in consciousness.

When souls are created out of infinite love, forged with God's free will, they are born to create and be, to create and give love. Now those souls who choose to experience, make a commitment to live that experience through and by God's laws.

When they choose the Earth's experience, each soul bridges all orders that make up Earth's experience—orders that are only known to God and the beginning and returned soul.

Now each portion that experiences through an order has free will thought to experience within that order and no other orders.

The human element projects personality born with free will to experience Earth's experience, to experience God's laws, to live God's love. There is more than one personality, generally speaking, projected upon Earth at a given period of time. These personalities rarely experience between themselves.

A personality may choose to pursue understanding. A personality may choose to pursue resolve. And there are many pursuits that a personality may pursue.

As the personality, the human personality pursues through thought, their experience, for on Earth the human personality, thoughts, and attitudes, are the key to their life and destiny on Earth.

They are also the key to the personality's just rewards on Earth and after or in-between experience. To understand another order, the animal order experiences telepathy and deals through sound. The animal order has that element of the soul as its greater self and its experience within the order most of the time necessitates experiencing the different animals on Earth.

That element may experience the power of a dinosaur or the beauty of a butterfly. It is a world of telepathy, sense, smell, and perception. It too is a thought projection confined to that order. The plant life has an element that projects within an order experience, the life of a tree, a flower, a fruit, the experience is vibratory and is emotional in that it is linked with the order of all consciousness, it is linked to love as all elements, orders, and consciousness are.

Now the human species experience different bodies, different colors, different sexes, different experiences, and in God's love is created equally with all elements of consciousness for they are all part of consciousness.

A human personality between lives may recognize that it is part of a greater self or exert its free will and deny that it is a part of a greater self. It can, with rest, create a projection or re-enter Earth's life. However, it comes to recognize that it does not have the sustained energy to recreate and seeks companionship to work with other personalities. When personalities find a part of the soul of their order, growth and understanding occur, and a path to God and love is journeyed marked by justice. The personality while between lives is learning. The application of what is learned is on Earth's experience if so chosen. But when projecting onto Earth or any experience God's law applies. Forged with free will is each element's free will to pursue the evolutionary path of love, God, and all that is.

Now there are degrees of understanding that advance one. It is not steps of a ladder or levels but for structural description or Earth, the meaning is the same. It is really like attracting like. On Earth, a football player and a housewife would have little in common and would not probably associate other than readings and pleasantry. The housewife would pursue interests probably with other housewives. The football player would pursue interests with other football players. The analogy is weak because we are not speaking of three-dimensional Earth but of the truth of shared reality. When one understands there is a natural progression to like-understanding and like-souls.

This law of like attracting like is operational on Earth, too. Opposites do not attract when brought together on Earth. There is a *just* reason and the attraction is one of justice.

When the personalities recognize the other parts of the portion of the soul that makes up the order of human species, advancement of understanding occurs.

When love is understood by a portion of the soul within the order of the human experience, then there is no longer the necessity to experience life on Earth, if justice has been resolved and truth understood. And truth being that love is God and God is love, that all are created equally and forged with free will by God and that all are a part of God.

Then the portion of this soul has found God. To be whole and complete in understanding within the Earth's planetary experience or solar system all portions of the soul meld together in understanding and love and grow and are with God. They may choose the Earth's experience as a walk-in or a savior or a leader or a housewife, whatever the experience the reason for their dropping in is for the betterment of mankind and they pursue love and understanding.

Now within the Earth's experience, the personality that is born onto Earth is born with free will. But as a projection of a greater self, it will in most cases be pursuing God, of course, but a vocation on Earth and the filling of *just* rewards for the soul. For what each human personality creates is a part of the soul.

The soul rejoices when love is given, and regrets acts of non-love. Each personality on Earth is at the particular part of life that they are because of their past thoughts on Earth and because of their soul's justice. Now what you are is what you have dreamed to be. If you dreamed to be a person of fear, then you are. If you dreamed to be a person of love, then you are. Fear grows when run from and disappears when faced.

Love never leaves; (it) is always a desire of the personality or soul and when pursued, grows. Love given grows and returns, they are the same as love received. You, as a personality, will receive what you give. If one chooses to give respect, they will receive respect. If one chooses to give fear, they will receive fear. If one chooses to give love, they will receive love. For what is given justly from the heart or mind or soul is returned always.

Each order on Earth rests, it can be hibernation for the bear, sleep for the human, dormancy for the plant, and so on. The rest in truth is the reality for all on Earth and they are the reflection of those dreams. Much of what one does is a reflection of dreams, some dreams recalled, others not. One's body and mind tell them when they are pursuing a negative path, for the body is an extension of the thought and when happy will look happy, when sad will look sad, when pensive will look pensive. The mind will tell it what to do.

We will add this portion to the book, there is more to add but this will be a small section.

Are there any questions?

Mike: No

Then we will conclude for this evening. Have a fine evening.

❀ SOUL AND THOUGHT

Tuesday, February 9, 1982, Session 112
This is a Wise One.

When the soul projects thoughts they project formless entities that are indeed forged with free will and that is just as the soul is forged with free will.

The soul creates various entities. Now when the personality is returning and transcends Earth's life it immediately, after a short transition period, returns to its level of understanding. A soul or fragment personality may not immediately understand that it has a Greater Self and may well search for a greater understanding of why it is no longer in physical and yet appears whole, and yet the soul visualizes in the soul's mind. Much of the early learning that takes place is understanding that the personality is not alone. That indeed it has a Greater Self. The personality before reincarnating again must find that Greater Self. It merely may be two personalities understanding that they are part of something greater.

When the soul projects upon Earth, it creates out of the combined knowledge of more than one fragment.

Many souls in a desire to quickly return to physical form do not take proper educational time to understand truth. Such souls focus themselves into physical reality and will live an unfulfilled life, for care has to be taken before entering the physical human body.

In a sense, it is like thrusting a little boy into a game before he understands what the game is about, what the rules are, and what the purpose is. Souls like that lead a very confusing life on Earth.

Now souls are essentially formless but can assume a form through thought. Souls have transparent bodies. Some, however, are not as transparent, for souls are marked by color and denser souls, more unlearned souls, are marked by heavier coloring. The color, in fact, does form matter. When souls project thoughts, those thoughts, where there are intent and purpose, are indeed with the soul for the remainder of its experiencing. A thought is a reality and a thought with intent and purpose can be very beneficial and very detrimental.

Wednesday, April 28, 1982, Session 162
This is a Wise One.

When creation occurs, any creation, be it from God and love given, or Satan and love held closely, it occurs from freely given thought. All creation, all beingness, all within, all create through thought and thought by all is freely expressed and can be changed only by the thinker.

There is a purpose behind every, every thought though that purpose may not be realized by the thinker or receiver. Even random thoughts have a purpose and are their freely given, though not always freely received.

Thought creates or dissipates energy. Action is a reflection of thought. Action is behavior psychologically speaking, motion, form, and substance (and) scientifically speaking, justice, creating, evolving, philosophically, religiously, metaphysically. The soul through evolution learns the laws of thought. A self-loving soul can master pretty much the physical laws of thought to a point of diminishing return.

All, all human behavior can be measured as a result of thought, love, justice, free will, and purpose. Thought is energy forming and energy absorbing. Thought creates electrical magnetical fields. Thought within what Earth knows as solid bodies or substances create electrical chemical action and frequency.

Thought is a part of all realities. Thought can and does change experience. A natural development of thought is imagery. Imagery is a perception for no two humans visualize and perceive in exactly the same manner.

Souls project and create through imagery. Each personality is an imagined personality by the projecting soul.

Thought in creating realities can and does form mass realities. Thought does form all realities but thought functions within orders, cycles, the evolutionary process, for is not thought the soul?

For example, elements that go up, or rather, that go to contribute to making physical bodies contain thought, love, and even free will, like the human personality, for they are a part of shared reality as all are. However, until elements understand their nature which is contained within their order, their process, their cycle, they remain bound to that order, cycle, and experience. When elements achieve total awareness, have resolved any justice, or have fulfilled their evolutionary duty to order, they remain in that order.

Thought is contributed by all, however, the human order does not perceive the thoughts in order that exists within the human body, just as trees do not perceive the thoughts of the human personality.

However, known or unknown all perceive the "physic or action" of thought in some manner or another.

There is an infinite number of cycles, orders, processes, contained within the total evolutionary process of the evolving soul. To explain the total process would take what Earth calls eons of time and then never fully be described, for thought is infinite.

However, understand this, thought creates all. The supreme thought is love given and love given is always forged with free will.

A love held closely, thought is always confined and limited and structured to the self's will and can never recreate.

We will now conclude. Are there any questions?

Mike: No, I have none, thanks.

❀ THOUGHT IN PHYSICAL REALITY

Friday, February 12, 1982, Session 115

This is a Wise One.

When one is in physical reality, one projects thoughts that do indeed create their individual destiny and multiplied times the mass of humanity it projects human destiny.

If mankind wants war, so they shall have it. If mankind wants peace, so they shall have it.

War is fought out of fear, peace is lived out of love and understanding. In a war-torn society where wars are fought for causes and believed to be just and right the most courageous are those who say peace.

This is not to say courage does not exist in wartime, for one does face certain fears and find it necessary to face them down, but one also reinforces a behavior pattern whether individual or mass behavior. If one wishes, believes, thinks, that they will not succeed then they will not. If one wishes, believes, thinks that they will succeed then they will. Each, whether through purpose or through response or through imagery, visualizes what they are to become. All of what one becomes, of course, is not simple in the mind, for one may have for reasons of justice or purpose selected a particular path. Mankind is one of the many species that exist within infinite consciousness. There are other systems of experience with many like man's and many not like man's.

❀ BALANCE OF THOUGHT

Thursday, April 29, 1982, Session 163

In thought, one casts forth many images which create energy, forms, or impulses. Now thought can create attitudes and can adjust attitudes. "Attitude" is a degree of understanding and acceptance and perception.

One with a positive gives off energy. One with a negative consumes energy. Likes, or rather opposites, have been said to attract. That is not necessarily true. A depressed or negative personality needs a positive personality on which to absorb life-giving energy. A positive personality through just development may associate and frequent negative personalities. A balanced personality gives and receives, is at peace, and has a greater degree of understanding.

Now balanced personalities are on different vibratory levels. Balance for one is merely acceptance.

Acceptance will come to all seekers. The way to balance is through love. When thought permeates existence it does so as energy. One can walk into a room, a depressing room, and feel drained or walk into a happy room and feel uplifted. Now color does play a part in attitude. However, color is recognized differently and perceived differently.

There have been tests on Earth about wearing certain colors. There are various reasons why color effects, or rather, affects the human personality. One reason is familiarity, an association from soulness with certain colors.

Another is humankind's interpretation of brightness and darkness and lightness and how it affects the thought process. There are certain colors to be understood as healing colors and if it is so understood, so it shall be.

Thought is a part of free will for if one could not think freely one would not be initiating thought. Love is giving, and through giving, wise ones understand that much is received. When one is giving, one is expressing the highest eternal thought.

We will now conclude.

✼ WHEN THOUGHT TRANSCENDS ALL FORMS

Wednesday, May 5, 1982, Session 166
When thought is projected within any reflected experience it is defined within ordered evolutionary development. When thought is projected within form, known as color or aura, it is defined and confined to like energy mass.

When thought is projected by co-creators with God, it is infinitely expanding and transcending all forms and all experience and given God's laws of creation, thoughts projected as soul, entities are initially defined by order, and through experience, evolve justly. And thoughts projected are the creative reality for souls; thoughts reflected are the perceptive reality for soul-fragments, and truth transcends all soulness, for all soulness is God unfolding and enfolding.

All thoughts, from the simplest to the more creative through imagery, run a cycle of what your scientists would refer to as motion. Motion cannot be understood by reflected learning. Motion can be understood by eternal wisdom. Reflective learning is a God-being or soul-evolving perception of limits and definitions of perceptions. And thought and motion usually do not change to the eye of an evolving soul. A more highly evolved soul may begin to fathom some of the wisdoms and truths of thought and the reality creativeness and multidimensionality of thought.

The responsibility and operational truths of co-creating with God on the "God Plains," requires an understanding of thought, love, and free will as well as evolutionary processes.

Saturday, June 12, 1982, Session 185
This is a Wise Guide.

When the soul is projecting through intent, the soul receives what the intention of the thought was. When it is carried out into action, it receives equal return of a similar intent and action. The soul intends when it has an intrinsic desire. When the soul is wise and is projecting love, the soul can also be creating for the reward of creating something that fulfills the desires and needs of the soul. The wisest understand that what is created from the heart, the honest integrity from within given freely to all, receives back the same multiplied many times. For love reverberates and grows when given freely.

Now when it is self-love and meant for the self, it receives in full measure what it has given, nothing less, nothing more, until understanding or justice has been returned.

That is all for this evening.

❀ THOUGHT AND THE HUMAN PERSONALITY

Tuesday, July 27, 1982, Session 208

For the personality, as greater selves, act as teachers for the soul and God acts as a teacher for highly evolved souls.

I AM THAT I AM, thought from the soul's projection is visual imagery creating circumstances many times doing that communicating in the dream world for the evolving soul.

Now each visual circumstance may be played out by more than one soul, or many souls. So, dreams suggest to the evolving personality actions based upon what the personality would define as preexisting images and memories emerge, images locked in the mind.

Now the personality may fight to maintain individuality and yet find in so doing confusion, lack of direction, lack of purpose, lack of understanding, for the personality alone can only recall those memories from its immediate life if they chose to block out other memories that can be or are brought to the surface. The personality is involved in the dream world and even comes to some agreement on the direction. Those personalities who draw only upon personality traits and upon nothing greater will respond and will react to a situation based upon its learning. This occurs primarily in a newer soul, although it can occur in a more seasoned soul.

Thought is brought to what we will define as the memory banks of the thought system, so going into a situation as a human personality there are very few chance encounters. Souls usually evolve together in many of these probable drawings or probable experiences beforehand. The soul acts then as a teacher for the personality, as greater selves act as a teacher for the soul, and God acts as a teacher for highly evolved souls.

So, the human personality may come across chance meetings, however, this is very unlikely.

Now the circumstances that occur, maybe just circumstances, giving or receiving a debt. However, over time the personality and the soul understand they're interrelated with at least each other.

Now the higher self of a personality is the evolving soul. The higher self of the evolving soul is and are entities. And the higher selves of entities are other entities until the soul reaches home or God.

In one manner or fashion, or another just, as it is necessary and desirable for the human to relate to and function with other humans, it is to relate and function with other souls, so it is that an entity relates and functions with other entities, ever-expanding realizing that all are a part of shared reality.

Now all communications between the aforementioned personality, souls, entities, and God are vibrationally tuned, which has been described as harmonized.

Now the truth in one's being is like the truth in all beings. The truth is always recognized in one manner or fashion. Though it is concealed for reasons of gaining understanding.

SYMBOLOGY *(Same Session)*

Through the evolutionary process, which goes on many levels at various understandings, various experiences, symbology—whether it be presented as structure, visualizations, or philosophy—represents common focal points by which to practice the art of creating and evolving.

In all systems of reality, there is symbology and yet even symbology must be personally interpreted and individually interpreted and agreed upon. Good and evil are symbolically related, acceptance and rejection are symbolically related, God and devils are symbolically related, and wisdom and magic are symbolically related. The word we meant to use in our previous relations example is symbolically.

Symbology is necessary when evolving and even souls who have evolved beyond all the souls must use symbology, agreed upon circumstance and structures by which to communicate ideas. As part of a God-given ability that exists within each, is the ability to think and the freedom to think and create what one chooses. However, through lack of understanding one may not always choose and respond in an understanding and loving manner according to the highest principles and yet may appear to respond in a very acceptable manner to those on Earth and other experiencing realities.

Though truth in terms of statements is really a very simple interpretation, does not always make it so, thought is truth, free will is truth, and love is truth. And the benefit of truth and the benefit of thought and love and free will expression is just.

Now, again symbolically speaking, selves and alternative selves are separated by vibration and perception for purposes of planning and organizing. Because of the reality of shared reality, many people, many souls, shift many thoughts or are not attuned vibrationally, picking up many thoughts and may pick up random thoughts, symbolic thoughts. This is very true when one is coming to grips with giving up the self for God even though that one would get the self and more back.

Now when one is seeking truth one always eventually must face the symbologies, must face the chaos and conflicts of overcoming the false perceived individual self to find the true related self. And yet when this is found one finds they have not lost their individuality but gained their freedom and become more, and yet lose nothing or the many other selves that exist as part of the soul.

The validity of symbology is only functional and accurate as is perceived. Truth since it cannot always be, or is sought from within, is presented in various different manner that the various evolving selves agree to accept.

We will now conclude.

✿ FREQUENCY OF THOUGHT

September 15, 1982, Session 235
This is a Wise One.

Thoughts are electrical magnetically and electrical-chemical in nature. Thoughts are transported through vibrational frequencies. Thoughts are of various frequencies and carry their own unique reality and validity.

Each thought that is programmed into a frequency or is cast forth into a frequency remains alive in that frequency as energy. The aliveness of thoughts is dependent upon the nature of the thoughts and the use of the thoughts. But thoughts remain alive until they no longer be of any validity to a particular frequency.

Now a thought's free will desire is to remain alive and survive and find like thoughts or find thoughts that will give it greater energy so that it will remain alive.

Ideas remain alive in this manner and are transported in this manner. However, a thought does not know of a Greater Self, for a thought that was created for a purpose, knows only that purpose and lives for only that purpose as a form and a quality of energy.

The thought is a creation of a soul or a reflection of a soul and stays with that element that created it until it is no longer necessary; for the thought to remain around that which created it, until the thought no longer has any validity to that which created it.

Thoughts remain though within the vibrational frequency by which it was created marked by energy and color.

The thoughts make up uncounted impulses that are and remain available for thinkers and beings of a like frequency.

An animal has its own brand of and its own vibrational frequencies just as the human does and all elements that go to make up an experiencing system. All thought returns to their level of creation and remains there forever. The thoughts then are mini creations that exist forever in a realm of their own unique creation.

The thoughts that remain in these vibrational frequencies are picked up and used, added to or cast off and not used, by entities that are of a similar vibrational level.

Now the thought as the thought does not hold the same energy level as the thinker and can never hold that same energy level. The thought itself can only hold its own known energy level until it finds other thoughts that are of a similar energy level.

To hang onto a thought will mean to hang on to a particular energy level for as long as the thought is hung onto. Thoughts are then of their own uniqueness and do remain alive.

However, like all creations, thoughts themselves become multidimensional within their own vibrational level. The thoughts change over creations evolving and become assessable and understandable to creations evolutionary time. Therefore, old thoughts are interjected into an experiencing system as the system cycles.

All systems cycle, for they were created to cycle. The measurement and understanding of various systems depend upon the attunement of the thinker. Thoughts even remain when the system is no longer functional to the needs of a particular evolving system.

Now since it has been said that God is a creator and God created all in God's image and that God and all are thoughts, something should be clarified here.

God is.

There is but one God and yet all that is, go to make up that God.

God created out of love and forged upon each free will.

Therefore, each that God created will return to God at the vibrational level by which each was created and remain there forever, infinitely, at one with God, and yet still possessed of all the qualities that instilled in it. The it, of course, is the soul. We add that here, so that thought itself does not become the sought, or the God.

The permanency of thoughts is dependent upon their own unique quality. Thoughts though, remain alive forever but are not always resurrected again depending upon the nature of those thoughts. Now thoughts remain alive and possess their own unique brand of free will and loving soul.

Each thought we point out returns to its own level of creation. You, as a thought, will return to your own level of creation and take with you only those thoughts that are of a proper vibrational frequency. The thoughts may return as memories as you, the thinker, traverse a system or a reality as a cycle of time. However, if the thoughts are not of the quality that your frequency can stand or tolerate than you will not enter that system, as if for some reason you do, you will not function as effectively in that system as one attuned to that system. The thoughts function clearly for the maintenance of that system and there are always changes as new thoughts are introduced. As new thoughts are introduced, those thoughts of a very unlike vibration drop away. The term opposites attract is not really accurate over time and through cycles.

Now all souls are aware of this reality and there are special entities and creations, souls if you will, who deal in the realms of thoughts. Their function is to coordinate those thoughts and direct those thoughts. Their function will be explained more fully at a later time but let it be said now that all existence is multidimensional.

Thoughts then cycle and are a part of the vibrational frequency in which and by which it was created.

Now some thoughts are picked up by evolving souls because they, the evolving souls, are looking for those thoughts and some thoughts are sent to the evolving souls because of just or purposeful reasons.

A soul or a reflection of a soul can only receive and accept those thoughts that are of a similar vibrational frequency.

The soul through its desire, will change and accept various realities and attune to that reality. The soul will only be given that which is valid or necessary to the experience.

We will now conclude for now.

God loves all.

Wise thought: All exists and yet is perceived and understood from a perspective.

THOUGHT AND REINCARNATION

Sunday, October 24, 1982, Session 254

Beyond reincarnation to the soul, the evolving soul, there is reincarnation. Living and experiencing again and again until awareness and fulfillment satiate the learning element of the soul. Beyond reincarnation though is that which is no longer being reborn. That which is, that which loves, *maya* occurs, the separation ends. Reincarnation is for the purpose of loving that which eternally gives.

Now reincarnation itself is for the purpose of justice. Justice is for the purpose of receiving. Reincarnation occurs in this method. Thought is projected. Each thought carries its own vitality and reality. Each thought is freely given. The reason that enlightened thinkers give frugally, seemingly so, is what is projected and given is given out of love.

Each thought directs itself to a level of vibration or frequency through the method of sound marked by color. This ultimate sound has been reflected as AUM (HUMMMM). And the color associated with this sound illuminates a white gold, like the flame of a candle that appears to be gold, but its points of burning or giving is white. Symbolically, fire has been thought to be the flame of life, the sun the giver of life, the sound the breath of life. The thought that is given, whatever thought is given, moves in motion and is returned at the vibrational level by which it was given, rather, at which it was given. There are certain laws relating to the cycles of each vibrational level. Some of these laws have been incorporated in the zodiac and cycles of change.

Thought then functions on many different levels and many different vibrations and each thought continues forever in time. Thought carries electrical magnetical and electrical-chemical realities within the various levels. When thought is cycling it remains within the vibrational level in which it was cast forever. Thought stays and remains as a living reality forever. Thought seeks like thought. Thought ties the evolving soul to it until the evolving soul lets it go and be. The evolving soul though will cling to thought, even what may be referred to as irrational thoughts, until it comes to understand that it no longer requires it. Remember that thought is a prelude to endeavor or experience. The endeavor or the experience follows the thought.

Thought then carries its own energy and gives off its own energy and will behave in certain predictable manners. When thought is projected, intent is the driving force. Thought always returns to the one projecting it. Thought is about each and each is thought coming together to form an experiencing reality that is always returned to the giver in a like and similar manner.

Now each element of God is created in a like manner. Created from pure love and thought as a creation freely given with intention of love and loving to create. Thought in an evolving cycle merges together to form various realities. Thought is focused in an ordered manner. Thought is always the current being, the being of now. The quality and pureness of thought are reached through understanding, which is reached through experience in an ordered fashion. Thought is given in many ways and forms many realities. Each knows within that they evolve through opposing thoughts. Opposing thoughts by nature create an eternal conflict. This is evolving.

That is all for now.

✿ THOUGHT AS EVOLVING NATURE *(Same Session)*

This is a Wise One.

In a greater sense, all that are focused within an evolving system, are pitted one against the other in thought. When one focused in the human body observes plants, animals, and the Earth and their own body, it observes various conflicting data. Some, it relates to, and others it doesn't. Thought then, by evolving nature, is chaotic, which when one is going through a change of thought, there is always chaos, for it is a shifting of knowledge and understanding, and even vibrational energy.

This in an evolving system is always true. Thought then is when understanding arrives, giving but not projecting, giving without desire and loving without desire. And yet one must learn how to think and discipline their thinking process until one reach awareness and naturalness flows. Thought always has free will about it, will always seek the manner that it was given and be returned in the same manner.

Within each then is God. Each perceives themselves as individuals and set apart and so it shall be until the decision is made to become the individual you truly are. God gave in pure love and created in pure love. God is just and will receive what God has given back in pure love. Evolving souls give in an interpretation of love. But evolving souls are, within their seed, thought that which created them and them that created truth and love and innocence.

Innocence has two phases of thought; innocence of knowing and not yet doing, but not yet understanding, with the other side being the innocence of understanding and loving in pure giving truth, forever. So, one has untried innocence and understood purity and innocence without blemish. This has been referred to as duality within the various interpretations.

Since thought in truth and in its highest understanding quality is love, then love is within everything and makes everything run peacefully and smoothly. In expressing duality, one speaks of God's will and mass will, right and wrong, fallen and not fallen. Until there comes a manifestation of love through thought and will, then duality is all that can be seen. The Christ and others have been lovers of all, no longer in conflict but in touch with their true selves.

Has not the Christ said, a*nd you too will do all these things and more?*

Thought is an inner occurrence, and duality is an inner occurrence, and truth is an inner occurrence. Thought forms the basis for all of mankind's reality. Thought forms the basis for all reality.

Now thought discussed in an abstract fashion does not hold vivid realities to each unique human being. Because, as has been pointed out, each view is from an individual perspective until the separation is over and atonement is made. First, there is a coming together of will and thought and yet that can never be the final measure of God. Love and thought cannot be the final measure of God. Will and love cannot be the final measure of God. It's approached through love and viewed through love.

To view truth through will, individuals add to it. To view truth through love, singularizes it and conceptualizes it. To view truth through love, lives it, which explains a truth from God to you, that is you; a love given is a love received, a love held closely is a love held closely. Thought is cyclic in nature. For that is the way God has ordered it and that is the way each ordered their thought. In thought runs a cycle that is always returned to the giver. What is given in love to all must be received by all and returned by all in some manner or fashion.

We will continue this discussion tomorrow evening. Before concluding, beloved Kathy, do you have any questions about anything?

Kathleen: No, I have none thank you.

Then you may go and relax.

WHAT LIES BEHIND ALL THOUGHT

Excerpt from Saturday, November 20, 1982, Session 274
This is a Wise One.

Behind all the thought lies the intention. In the broader sense thought makes up the one in the three of God, for thought is. But that is not the defining aspect of God or of any being of God.

There is the will aspect or the expression aspect, and there is the love aspect or the giving aspect. In surveying or being a part of the "multidimensionality" of thought it can be defined various different ways for various different purposes.

Thought is, but is not, the defining quality of a being any more than just love is, as just will is. The three make one and the one is three in the will of God, which is that to create (through the use of thought), to give freely of the being self, expecting nothing in return and yet receiving the return; this is the will of God. It goes beyond thinking about the self or thinking about others. It is the truth, a truth that cannot be appropriately expressed in words but is at the essence of every thought being, every being.

Using an analogy of the human being—as a child, your body of thought or thoughts were not what they are now, nor will they be when you are older or even focused out of the human world, but the fact (is that) thought still will be valid. You will still be valid. Your intentions and thought quality will be measured through truth as will happiness, peace, and fulfillment. Creating is a part of your thought process. Love is a part of you. Therefore, both are a need and a part of you forever. Will is a part of you. Your will is to survive as an individual. God's will is that you will with all, as a part of all contributing and a part of all. That through all, and with all, is your salvation and your destiny. Share. It is your will against others or your will in line with God's will. Truth is thought, love and will.

THE HIGHEST QUALITY OF THOUGHT *(Same Session)*

This is a Wise One. We will continue.

The highest quality of thought is love and to give love freely is the will of God. To give love for your personal gain is your will. Truth is God. If there was not God within and available to each being than thought and creativity for the self would be a self-destroying endeavor. The power of thought often referred to is all the powers that have been spoken of. Thought is powerful. It has gotten you exactly where you are in the evolutionary process. Thought has created and destroyed worlds and civilizations. In the greater sense there is not good and evil, for God does not view it so. God has created each out of thought of love—the light of love—giving each then free will, thought, and love.

That bequeath of God that each created in God's image should receive in full measure what is given, (created) through thought is a double-edged sword. A thought given is a thought received. Give in thought what you wish to receive. That is the giving and receiving of thought. Both are one. A love held closely is a love held closely. That is the suffocating of thought. It has been said and rightly so that God can work with doers. Those who live and endeavor and do, and not work with those who sit tied in fear that if they do not give a thought, they can commit no act that they can be held accounted for. Of course, there is no advance or improvement in happiness. There is a building of fear though.

Now within the bodies of consciousness, there are of course like vibrational frequencies that contain a full complement of positive and negative. Yes, there is positive and negative within like vibrational frequencies. Positive and negative is not good and evil in the world of thought. These bodies of thought will only function within the human world in a cyclic fashion referred to as wheels within wheels in various forms of literature. Within the world of consciousness are beings and like some humans who sleep in the evening and work and play in the day, there are cycles of this for these beings, too.

NOTE: Coordinating points are points of agreement. They can be positive or negative, or they can be in (rare) circumstances both positive and negative or even non-charged. Coordination points are points of entry and of leaving of a system when thought leaves and enters. Now these points themselves are not all stable. Some cycle and change in interrelation with other cycle systems and other dream "realities" both larger and smaller. Some are more stable and yet much harder to discern since they cannot be arrived at or followed alone. They are the points of transition between "dream realities" of vaster nature. They are known by advanced beings only. The knowledge, though, is not through an accumulation of knowledge but an understanding and awareness of truth principles. These principles are of course the "laws" or the functioning truths that guide systems. All systems contain multidimensional realities and yet the operational laws that govern each system and being are simple. In the statement or supreme and basic truth of "a love given is a love received" is explained (as) thought, quality of thought, and basic and supreme will of thought. From here all other laws and rarities have been created. (Again, positive and negative is not good and evil but energy realities forming various bonds and anti-bonds.) Science knows of this from an earthly perspective to greater and lesser degrees.

Thought is then both outside and within the reality of the Earth and the living human. Various individuals have received communication from a greater reality or another reality than themselves to varying degrees. Those who have experienced communication from other beings have always and will always have varying degrees of difficulty in describing thought and reality because words and meanings have so many different connotations. Even images do, for is not another thought based upon your perspective? It cannot be stressed strongly enough that at its base, thought is creative in nature. The creative element of thought is the free part of thought not as strongly constrained by fears and guilt and accumulation of nonessential knowledge. Hence, in describing thought one seems to be going about in circles with no absolute line of development, for it is multidimensional. Each description is based upon inner understanding and observation such as it is. When God said the word, you can defend without fail, that is an absolute truth with not a set line of development, for there are many universes, but for God's endowment to each soul—what is given, is.

THE PARADOX

Monday, November 22, 1982, Session 276
This is a Wise One. We will begin with a paradox.

A soul is thought and yet not thought. This paradox can be described in this way. At a soul's basic being is a creative instinct. A creative desire manifested through will, which is expression. And indeed, a soul does create. That simply explains the beingness of a soul as they enter a system such as Earth's universe and as they leave a system such as Earth's universe. (Of course, it is not Earth's universe, but a universe of which Earth is part of.)

Why then would a soul enter a system wanting to create through will the expression and leave the same system a creator through expression and will? That paradox lies in the law of creation. That paradox defines, or rather brings into a need, for definition. And that is the quality of creation. A creator then creates, but for what reason; for the reason of happiness and fulfillment, for to be a creator and not to express, brings no joy or fulfillment.

When expressing (and) implementing the will, a soul begins upon the journey of learning to be happy through creation. Now thought is connected to creation for it creates. It is the word to describe that which a creator uses to create a tool of creation. Masters of our universe guide the creative instinct through the thought process. The instinct is to create. The tool is thought. The created or manifested ion is thought. All that is within the universe to which the Earth belongs was created. It was created by thought and is a thought of the creator. But to observe creations does not explain the quality or the joy of creation. The quality of creation has a distinct association with love.

That which marries and binds creativity, thought and will, is love. The reason why thought is the manifestation is because thought is that which is received and given from the creative instinct. Without thought, the creator would not be creating or using instinct nor using will and expression. Quality and love simply describe that element of thought that determines whether a soul can use the tool of thought or be used by the tool of thought. Thoughts held, bind or limit creative abilities. Thoughts give and return, but if held again they limit and bind the creator.

Now the soul entering a system knows this but has not learned to use the tool of thought. A soul leaving the system understands, or better understands, how to use the tool of thought through creativity and that is through love, which is the word used to describe giving. For a love given is a love received. The paradox of love is a love held closely. It represents the learning aspect of creativity and is thought and yet is not thought. The Lord God is a creator, and each has been created as a soul to be a creator. Now thought itself, the tool of creation, is multidimensional. It can be used in joy or can create destruction. Much like nuclear physics creates vast amounts of energy that can be used for good if not contained but directed and given, or can be used destructively if contained within a shell-like bomb potentially exploding and affecting all about it. Accept that life is eternal so nuclear physics is merely an analogy to describe a tool that can be used and misused.

That will conclude for tonight.

POSITIVE AND NEGATIVE THOUGHT

Notebook #28, Page 6
In the nature of everyday events, one is in a wakeful dream world. This dream world involves a communication technique of thought projection as well as verbal projection. The thoughts that one individual personality thinks are all about one and when directed toward a life form, they are all about that life form.

Now thoughts can be accepted or rejected depending upon the nature of the projector and the projected to. Thoughts are usually found in like personalities or like souls. Each thought of intent is valid and does achieve a destination. But since the nature of all created is a thought of love, thoughts that are not of love, though felt by the intended, boomerang and effect and bind and depress the projector or thinker of those thoughts. This is often reflected in a bitter or "poor me" personality.

Now all of us have had thoughts such as these in our life on Earth and to the extent that one thought negative, then we create for ourselves a less fulfilling time of our Earthly life. To the extent that those thoughts are positive, we create a much happier and fulfilling life on Earth.

Thoughts that project upon other forms when they are of love, aid those life forms as well as yourself. They, in fact, are returned manifold to you the sender. Thought that is projected upon life form or fellow humans that is of intent and not out of love can have varied effects. If the thought falls upon a like-soul, then that soul will receive that negativity and return it manifold resulting in a negative atmosphere around all involved. Each of you has walked into a situation when you could feel the air around you filled with goodness or depression. One can project a negative thought or intent upon a positive soul, and it will literally bounce back to the sender. All life forms around one feel the positive love and the negative fear and respond accordingly. All life form yearns, seeks, desires and requires love for that is the seed of the order by which all life forms are linked.

Through love, you are your natural self. Love given is the law of God, the truth of creation. That is natural and most creative. Psychologists, psychiatrists, doctors, and therapists, have in your time treated what is wrong or perceived wrong with life forms. If the approach to the situation was to look for what is right, then one would seek through love and look for the response to love. That exists as a part, the part of all. This approach accomplishes many positive cures, both for the therapist and the patient.

Love is the order by which all are equal in God's eyes.

THE SUPREME THOUGHT

Notebook #30, Page 9
This is a Wise One.

Thought is reality that is shared by all and all contribute to thought. The only infinite reality that can be created is through love. Love is the supreme thought, the truth. When creating out of love one creates a free will element of God that expresses through experience by order and justice.

Experience created by thought.

Creation is through thought of love forged with free will.

Justice in one's soul determines experience through order that is understanding of God's laws. Love all equally. Love for love, not for others interpretation.

GOD'S LAWS AND CREATION

*God created soul out
of the 'thought' of love.*

*Creation is an ongoing process.
It is always out of love.*

CHAPTER 5

GOD'S LAWS AND CREATION

The following thought-provoking sessions explore the creation of Earth, solar systems, humans, animals and souls, and discusses their forged free will—all in this shared reality and all created out of the 'thought' of *love*, emphasizing that God is Love and that love is the method of attaining wisdom and is the way of all.

The sessions speak of how we have co-created with God all along and we are never alone. That the laws of God are our laws because we have co-created them. Within this chapter, God also speaks, at which time my father was instructed to draw the face that you see on the cover of this book.

So, come sit with us.
These messages are meant for you.

(DICTATION BEGINS)

✿ GOD CREATED SOUL

Notebook #10
This is your Wise Guide. You will now write for the book.

God created soul out of the 'thought' of love. Soul is a 'thought' of love. God created the energy out of a 'thought' of love. The energy is a 'thought' of love. God created energy as a form for the soul, for God is total energy. Energy is a sound converted into color. All are part of the creative evolutionary process. God is All, All is God.

God created all energy and is all energy. Energy is of love, the thought, soul, sound, and color. Energy is the continuing creative process by which all continue to create. Energy is that which created and hold together your world, your solar system. When the souls no longer desire a solar system, such as Earth, and its planets on which to experience, then it will disappear just as quickly as it was made to appear.

✿ FRAGMENTS OF PERSONALITIES *(Same Session)*

This is your Greater Self. Your/our reincarnations are grouped into fragments. Say, if there are eighteen fragments on Earth at the same time, then they represent one incarnational personality. So, when we say we are Bach *(Johann Sebastian Bach, the composer)*, we are, but we are other fragments at the same time. When going back, forward, and now to read incarnational personalities we take the strongest personality that best represents the purpose for the incarnation or we take the most known personality, or relate a fragment to another known Earthly personality.

When this is done, the incarnational personality is contributing to the whole essence and the essence is contributing to the God portion and to all since all are a part of God and God is a part of all.

This is God.

Mike drew a big drawing of the face as seen on the cover of this book.

Love is understanding that all is God and God is All. That all were created equally in the eyes of God.

Mike is doing the writing now on the tablet. "A note to myself. Acceleration, velocity, sound, color, energy. Energy is in part and in whole all of these components plus that greatest component of all, God, and all that God is and that is All."

Mike is writing on the tablet in big writing.

"This is God. Your creative juices are flowing."

CREATION AND FORGED FREE WILL

Notebook #15, Page 10

This is a Wise One. We will now talk of creation.

Creation is that which all have created. Events are created through mass thought. The thought of Earth and its solar system is an example. The thought of a political belief changing is another example. Thought can move man to do what is seemingly impossible. It all starts with a thought. Creation is thought transformed into energy. This thought on Earth manifests itself to its accomplishments through resolve.

This is your Wise Guide. We will now talk of creation. Now, remember that creation is of God, All That Is, I Am that I Am, or any name that represents a creative force that creates out of love. Now the reason for the so-called evil souls, and they do exist to the extent that they are ego-oriented to the point that they consider themselves individually powerful creators. All too, exist at once, infinitely, just as there is no beginning, no end, just infinite existence.

There has always been individually forged free will upon, or as a part of, the soul. This forged free will is that we are all a part of God and God is a part of us all. That each is a co-creator, but not individually a creator. That creation is out of thought and that thought is good and out of love, souls are good and are of good thought.

Creation is an ongoing process. It is always out of love. The soul does absorb all its learning and can choose to accept or reject it, but all souls are of good and of love. Understanding love is the key, for as has been said, 'love is the clause.'

Monday, November 2, 1981, Session 36, 9 P.M.
This is a Wise One. We will now talk of creation.

Creation is a process of thought. Creation is a process of love. Creation is a process of need. Creation is a process of evolution. Evolution is a process of learning. Evolution is an infinite process of being. Evolution is a process of evolving to understand all that is; all that is, is God and God is all that is.

Good evening. This is a Wise One. Creation is a thought of love from God. God is all. Human beings are a creation of genetic evolution. The human body cannot exist without a portion of a soul. Without a soul, there is no human, for humans and all about humans are thought.

Earth and solar systems are a process of natural or nature's evolution. However, earth and solar systems are a thought of souls. If there was no need for the Earth experience, there would simply be no Earth.

Earth and solar systems are separate from the evolutionary process of humans, but they are part of all and are a part of shared reality. The Earth will give you what you give it.

Animals are a process of evolution. They, too, have a genetic evolution. They, too, are a thought. They have no free will. They evolve in balance with nature. Animals were made by the thought from free will souls. That which souls create must complete an evolutionary process.

Mankind must give to all as part of understanding Love.

This is a Wise, Wise, Wise One.

Love is the method of attaining wisdom. Love is a way of all.

Wednesday, January 13, 1982, Session 91
This is a Wise One. We will now speak of creation.

When a soul is created it is forged with free will. Souls are created by All That Is, I Am That I Am, Infinite Supreme Consciousness, God. Supreme consciousness does manifest itself or portions in any experience and creates any experience through thought. With each created soul supreme consciousness becomes grander, larger. This has been going on infinitely for there is no time in thought. Thought is its own past, present and future, shifting at will, thinking and creating in the present, past and future, changing, recreating.

Now when a soul is created through thought it is forged with love and free will and thinks independently. Yet the nature of creation is such—the nature of love is such—that to think out of love *given* creates a larger more beautiful grandiose element or soul of God. Love *taken* gradually diminishes the energy within that soul.

Now there are infinite experiences. Earth is a speck of time in the infinite variety of experiences that souls of enlightened nature can experience. In all, experiences are created by thought, for God is one soul that we are a part of.

Now supreme consciousness, that consciousness or element within the total consciousness that has the full range of creative ability through its understanding and practice of love, creates not just souls experience and co-creators but creates many other elements out of love.

These other elements are created for an order of development and have within their order free will and complete understanding of love. They serve to function within an order just as souls that manifest personalities function within an order.

Now, these other orders of consciousness, in fact, have their own systems, their own relationships, communications, families if it's within the nature of the order. They do not have levels of development that are mentioned in mankind literature, they do not have books and conveniences and they cannot create, such is the nature of their order. And yet the soul through thought, creates and co-creates, through thought all other orders, forging them within an order with free will. And no order is greater than the whole and the whole is no greater than the smallest part.

Such is the nature of creation and love. These other orders, life forms, both seen and unseen to the human eye, exist out of thought but are not thinking orders themselves.

❀ HOW MIRACLES EXIST *(excerpt from Notebook #15, Page 10)*

Mike: What about miracles?

Yes, they do exist in terms of human development. They can cure disease, they can inspire change, they can heal soul, bodies, minds. Miracles, as all, start from an understanding from within.

Understand that you are all a part of God and have co-created with God and have co-created with God all along, that you are not alone ever, unless you wish to be, that justice does exist and that there is some order to all. That the laws of God are your laws, for you have created them in the understanding that love is the supreme thought. Love is the thought of creation, that the souls of all are very wise and supreme in the sense that "one" alone does not change the world or thought. For example, I will write a great book to explain to the world creation, the evolution of soul. That book is a joint effort that is being contributed to by all, even the so-called evil as a part of all, are contributing their thought.

This is your Wise Guide. You may go now. We are always with you.

(Same Session, Notebook #15, Page 10)
This is God.

God of all loves all and contributes to all. Each is a part of all and all is a part of each. In truth, each will see that God, All That Is, I Am That I Am, is a part of each and a truth that is infinitely, infallibly, undeniable.

You do not worship the sun. The sun is a part of all that is as you are—a part of all that is. The sun is a power source, a natural power source. The energy within the sun is available to all. The energy within the sun has the power necessary to fuel and run all the earthly things that need power. The human body needs the source of thought, of love to rejuvenate. The sun is not to be worshiped for it is not a God but a part of all that is.

GOD'S LAWS

Saturday, November 21, 1981, Session 54
This is a Wise One.

One of God's Laws is (to) love all. Love all, greatly.

One of God's Laws is all are created equally in the eyes of God.

One of God's Laws is (to) accept what you cannot change and change what you cannot accept.

One of God's Laws is justice in your heart you shall have.

One of God's Laws is resolve and you shall find.

One of God's Laws is love for the reward and you may have the reward, love for the endeavor and you shall find the love and reward.

One of God's Laws is (to) have faith in yourself and you will have faith in God.

Have faith in others and you shall have faith in God.

One of God's Laws is (that) souls are forged with free will.

One of God's Laws is (that) Love is infinite and infallible.

GOD LOVES ALL.

THE HUMAN BODY AND PERSONALITY AS SOUL

When the child is born,
a new personality is born
and charged with free will.

When one is born into Earth's experience,
one assumes the challenges of the human personality.

THE HUMAN BODY AND PERSONALITY AS SOUL

In the very beginning of Earthly life, soul makes the decision to transfer into the human body. Soul then gives life to the human body. This chapter explores how and when soul comes in and the various crucial elements that make up the human body, the purpose of a soul's decision to enter, and how then thought, free will and the growth of the evolving personality must work in unison with all other elements. Among various subjects, Wise Ones come forth to offer love, intelligence, and detailed descriptions of the relationship of thought and personality, 'bad' people and 'bad' deeds, forgiveness, mercy, and inevitable justice.

So, come sit with us.
These messages are meant for you.

(DICTATION BEGINS)

✿ THE HUMAN BRAIN

Monday, November 16, 1981, Session 49 – Excerpt
This is a Wise One. We will talk of the human brain.

The human brain exists without the mental body of the soul. The human brain will respond to stimuli and reflex action for as long as it has blood. However, without the mental body of the soul, the human brain will not function as you know it today. The operation of the human body is dependent upon the soul which is a part of the whole body, permeating the whole body. The mental body of the soul records the human experiences of everyday living and it goes with the mental body of the soul and is a part of the soul or essence. All thoughts are recorded within it and must be dealt with.

The human body has a soul body or essence as a part of it. It exists as a part of the human body for as long as the human body is living. There have been cases when a soul did not understand the relationship between the human body and tried to remain with it and make it live once more. However, this is rare and only happens with a soul that does not understand that the soul is the life, the body merely a temporary room for an overnight stay. This could take place in a more elementary form of life but does not because of other forms of life's limitations.

The human body as a generic term is one of many bodies that the soul may use to fulfill a reincarnational experience. There can be many bodies at once in a given incarnation.

✿ HUMAN RESPONSE MECHANISMS

Thursday, December 3, 1981, Session 64
We will speak of the human response mechanisms.

There is a connection between energy and the body. The energy being the soul and all that is about the body. There is an inner relationship between energy forces which is why one can feel highly charged or very bogged down or dragged down in certain areas or as well as certain individuals.

The connection is a conversion process between blood cells, brain cells, marrow, and nerves. One has the ability to heal another when they understand the relationship. Now when this connection or transfer takes place, blood flows, organs function, impulses are sent from the brain, and of course, the body works. Without this, the body dies.

✿ TRANSFER OF SOUL AND THE HUMAN FETUS *(Same Session)*

When a transfer is made, it can be made at birth in the fetus through the umbilical or it can be made in an exchange in later life. When it occurs at birth there is an adjustment process that takes place between energy and the functioning of the human body and the developing egg and fetus. It is all a very ordered system, the human body. The human body has a genetic process, as does all life, wherein certain things can be transferred from generation to generation. Their eyes, skin, but not—not—not intelligence. Intelligence is a soul-learned thing based upon the evolutionary process of the soul and upon what a soul learns in a given experience. All life is energy. And energy is from thought and is converted to elements and life. Therefore, it is natural that energy that is created by the souls and God and converted to elements and life works best for all.

We will now let you rest. Do not worry about your father. You already know he is making the transfer gradually over to this side. Have a good evening.

(Kathleen Speaking) They must have been referring to my father who passed in 1976 and came through and spoke through Mike a few times.

Notebook #38

When the soul is incarnating in the human body through the process of visualization, there is a gradual change in frequency, vibration, and pitch of the soul as a whole entity that includes all aspects of soulness.

Now within the order of the human being, there is awareness of this reality, but not a total awareness until the soul comes in fuller contact with itself. The soul transforms itself into a quiet meditating nonactivity state within the soul mind.

Now while this is being done by the soul, the human body is conceiving and being formed based upon the genetic history of the family and species and the order of the human physical species. The body muscle, bone, organ, skin and all that goes to make up the body are formed, at present, by what your scientists refer to as reproduction. Although there is still much to learn about this process in general, it can be said that physically speaking, that is how the human body is formed.

Now the body itself cannot function within society without the soul focusing a free will personality in the physical human body. This is done through, as we have said, imagery and visualization and love. The love we speak of is the functional multidimensional love of all that is and the laws of love that is a truth for all, accepted or realized or not.

Now while the fetus is forming, the soul may decide not to enter the body until after the fetus has formed or may decide to enter while the fetus is forming. The reasons for choice remain with the soul and its development within evolutionary concepts of truth. The soul then decides that it will enter into the human endeavor and species, known as man or mankind for purpose, love, understanding, evolution, creating, and order. A soul is then at last in Earthly time focused as a free will entity with the human body known as a personality. The soul focused within this personality realizes its place within order and its ability and requirement to direct and take care of that body.

Now the body itself can be or probably is not a part of the soul itself but the soul is focused with that order, too. As the soul and body develop, there is a period generally thought to be seven years (seven is a number of significance and reference on Earth) when the personality begins to assume its soulmanship and personalityship.

Now the evolving personality deals with and functions within the ideals, structures, philosophies, and lives of humanity, and deals with reality from that viewpoint. However, the evolving personality also is intrinsically connected to a Greater Self, generally referred to on Earth as a subconscious, but for sure a higher concept. The personality then goes through life after life dealing not only with ideas and concepts of mankind but understanding deep-seated thinking that is sometimes at conflict with what the soul personality sees going on about itself. In dealing with this, the soul will automatically go through various internal conflicts with the soul-self and the personality and outside observations. The personality, in almost all situations on Earth, is the perspective from which we as evolving mankind deal with and through. This personality to become qualified as sane by mankind learns to deal from what is acceptable to the tenants and beliefs of the current civilization and/or culture. Shifts from area to area and idea to idea (church, state, society, etc.) require adjustment.

The personality throughout its life learns to adapt and function adequately within the human endeavor according to pervading current beliefs then. But throughout the process of life, the personality is connected with the soul as a part of order. Now when the soul is allowed to speak, there may and almost always is that internal conflict with which we have spoken. The soul cries to express itself through the personality, to allow the personality to understand that it is not alone in its endeavor on Earth. The personality who accepts this after a while becomes a charged personality.

Now the complexity in describing this process of evolution from the standpoint of the evolving human personality would involve too many analogies and examples and would further confuse the evolving personality. The most simplistic way of explaining this process is through creation, evolution, God, and truth. The personality, as everything, is part of all that creation, is of God. God is All. Evolution is of God. God is All. God is that human word used to describe the highest beingness.

Truth is love, thought, and free will.

The personality may not understand what is going on outside of itself but each can accept that the "I" that they know within exists as thought, and that within they have the right to accept or reject any thoughts that the "I" does not accept. To try and measure what another evolving personality is doing and judge that by what many others are doing, tells the personality that it is a little different or a lot different from those that the personality is viewing.

Each individual personality will think and will think as freely as it knows how or has evolved to understand. But each personality is a thinker and creates its reality through that thought and freely interprets and comes to the best understanding it can from within. Each personality then creates and evolves as it wishes, based upon the understanding that exists within.

Now each of us can accept that we think and each of us to some degree can accept that we can freely think, but what has been lost is the understanding and power of that thought, and what is always sought of course is the quality of that thought.

For me to say that each has created its own destiny says nothing to the personality who is locked in a deformed body and is struggling to eat and survive day to day, so accurate observations cannot be made from the viewpoint of the individual personality or even the individual seeking soul. And so, mankind knows that there is indeed something greater than its individual selves and its mass selves and that sometimes has been Gods or God. We as evolving personalities and souls do not understand the magnitude of God but accept, for we really have to, that there is indeed something greater than the "I".

So, in dealing with our own personal realities we always have to come back to the understanding that what we "think" of, we internally perceive.

So, we look to God, and in so doing we do express God's image. God thought the world into being in all its forms and realities and created all equal in God's image. Thought, free will, and love. For what greater act of love can one give but to allow each infinite freedom to create. And in one form, manner, or another, is not love that we all seek and express? There lies the quality of love, God, thought, and free will which we admire, write about, sing about, and revere in many forms. Is there a better way of describing God than love? And all the great ones that we honor here on Earth, do we not ascribe love to them?

So, the personality reads and tries to adhere in some manner and form to precepts of love, but seemingly sees many contradictions to love operating outside its own self. Finally, for most of us, we come to that feeling or emotion within that says, "where is the justice in this world, for if everyone else would start to love then so would or could I." This concept does not apply to all of course, but in the process of growing up have we all not asked where the justice in this world is, or the justice in our own particular lives is?

To state it bluntly, justice is in God and God is All. The All that I speak of incorporates much more than Earth or Earth's universe, it incorporates infinity. And what do these higher concepts and teachings tell us? In one way or another, a love given is a love received. A love held closely is a love held closely. There in love lies justice, what we give so shall we receive.

For example: If you judge so shall you be judged. If you forgive so shall you be forgiven, and the truth of justice goes on infinitely from then and to there. Innate within each of us lies the understanding, desire, and truth of love. It is not up to the next guy, but up to each of us to create the brotherhood which we all talk of. "Do unto others as you would have them do unto you." For they will.

Now the personality feels this within and expresses it through understanding, justice, order, and love.

Monday, December 28, 1981, Session 79

This is a Wise Wise Wise One. Are there any questions?

Mike: I'd like to ask a question about the human when ... my understanding that the soul by choice enters a human body from birth.

You wish to understand the nature of an evolving human personality and its relationship to a Greater Self.

The soul sends out many fragments, those that enter the human from birth, on doing so choosing parents and time and place of birth. This accounts for those pregnancies that are early or late. The fetus understands when it wishes to be born. The seeking of time, place, and nature of birth is done with justice *(and love)* in mind and with purpose in mind. Now when a soul enters the human body, the agreements are such that a personality is chosen based upon probabilities, purpose, and justice *(karma)*.

Now the human personality, if it refuses to acknowledge the Greater Self and the purpose and chooses to think self-unique, will choose events to fit the benefit of the human personality based upon probable choices, circumstances, and reaction. These choices determine a path for the justice will be had and new justices may be created. The purpose may be ignored, and the soul will eventually return to this side to understand and learn what its errors were and what it must accomplish. Now there are many fragments to a soul, and each one forever, a personality, each one seeking to return to the Greater Self, when all fragments understand the nature of the experience and understand the Greater Self, then there is no longer a need for Earthly incarnations.

Now more highly evolved souls have, so to speak, accumulated more of their fragments and therefore have more understanding of the nature of God, All That Is, and Love. Now the soul or the Greater Self understands more, much more than any single fragment. A fragment will continue to exist on this side seeking to find purpose and meaning until it finally accepts the Greater Self and becomes part of the Greater Self and accepts the Greater Self forever.

Now the Greater Self may send out other fragments and those fragments have a direct link to all other fragments that exist as part of the Greater Self. All of the experiences are part of the Greater Self. Now in the highly evolved state a soul may send out a fragment into an adult human being who wishes to give up the Earthly life for one reason or another and there is an agreement, for they must be agreed, and an exchange is made. For lack of a better term, we can call these souls "walk-ins." When a soul enters another human body, that personality retains all its memory and a portion remains with the body, the exchange is made with the mental body only, not the casual body; the mental body is the Greater Self.

That should answer your question sufficiently? Do you have any more questions?

Mike: Was Jesus a walk-in?

Yes, the soul or fragment Jesus was part of a highly evolved soul. An Avatar, who understands his mission. The spirit of Christ the Lord entered into the man Jesus during the final years of his life to fulfill prophecies, to create love, to speak the word of the seed of love.

Mike: Are there many avatars?

Yes, they are all not working exclusively on Earth. Your question about what next after Avatar will be dealt with more fully later.

Mike: How many souls contain a human body?

It depends on the level of understanding of the soul. Certain highly evolved souls can have many souls within them at a given time of need and purpose. But only for the benefit of all, never for self-benefit.

Mike: I don't have any more questions for now.

Then you may go and have a good evening.

Wednesday, November 10, 1982, Session 267

When the fetus is being formed, it is formed from the positive and negative egg. Symbolically only this refers to the positive male and the negative female, the positive father, the negative mother. Earth symbolically is the mother, the Sun is the father. We have only stressed this is symbolic only. The reality is the electrical magnetically attraction that forms matter in varying degrees.

From the formation of the fetus formed out of fluid in the sac, as all is formed out of a vapor converted to fluid, gas, converted to fluid, the fetus begins to take on form. The process is one of electrical magnetical and electrical-chemical assimilation and growth that eventually forms a human body and all of the various organs. The formation of this human body is developed from life-giving processes and cells within the female. We speak of the human body here. There is a conversion from liquid to matter, vapors to matter that is occurring. Measurements of electronic vibrations would change during the birth cycle or formation cycle of the fetus. This is a miniature form of creation in terms of forming matter. The system is already in place in the human body. This is genetically true regarding the formation of a human body. However, the reason for the formation has nothing to do with birth control and abortion, but the evolution and placement of souls for the expression of learning of God.

As a quick general statement:

Births are agreed upon in the thought state between all participants. When the human body is delivered as an infant that process of the human, orders, souls, focusing begins. The child that is developing is developing physically and is developing the personality which it came to develop. The relationship of the human body and personality of the soul relates to planetary influences also, to be a complete system.

Beyond all forms and manifestations is the thought process which uses the elements of the system to create and to form. All systems including the human body are meant to function perfectly without disease or illness. There is a smooth flow of fluid with an electrical current, which flows through the body. In very ancient times there were races where food was not required. The body was sustained on the naturalness of the environment and the thought was able to transport the body easily. Each organ and each cell and element within the human body are perfectly designed. There are within the human body focal points or coordination or pressure points as there are within any system that is directly related to the flow of the universe. The inner relationship exists in a variety of ways.

Physical man is contracted of the same elements to greater or lesser degrees that are within the physical Earth. The triggering mechanisms that form bodies into the matter that it does, is a *just* system. For within the system there are better times of entry for souls, or more optimum times, that would allow a smoother communication between the soul and human being/personality focused in matter.

The human body triggers off the appropriate electrical magnetical formation to form another human being which will receive in its body, and during and through the proper points the developmental aspects of the human personality.

✿ HEALING WITH HANDS, CRYSTALS, AND HYPNOSIS

Sunday, December 20, 1981, Session 77
This is your Wise Wise Wise Wise Wise One Guide. We will now speak of healing. Healing and how it is done with the hands.

Man is made up of atoms and molecules that do, of course, form energy. These atoms and molecules are in constant motion and do in fact put together physical beings of man. These atoms and molecules are ever changing and when in balance are able to move about and communicate with other atoms and molecules. This is done when one is in tune with nature.

Now not all realize that they have this ability, but by touching and transferring with thought, the thought of healing another group of atoms and molecules can be restructured to begin or actually heal. The method by which this is accomplished is through thought. So, the receiver has to be willing to receive so the healing can be accomplished.

Now to say that the patient must think well in order to become well is true, however, with a known technique one can heal another body and that body can still become healed and yet lose the patient. So, when healing with the hands, one must set a sequence of thought that is acceptable to the patient. This may take some time, but one's intuition will know when the patient is ready to receive this healing.

The greatest healing that you will do will be healing of the soul and the psychic and realigning the thought of mankind so the knowledge springs forth that nature provides all healing, that the body has natural healing attitudes, and working in concert most sicknesses will be eliminated.

Now this will not come about immediately, even though it is right and it is best for the mind and for the body of all, for your medical sciences will fight this as they do now. They will perceive that one will be saying that everything they have accomplished went wrong when, of course, it is not. The medical profession, the physician, is there for the healing of the total man.

Another form of healing that will come into practice will be healing crystals with the use of light, heat and color. This will come to be an accepted method of practice as it was during the time of Atlantis.

And still another form of healing will be through hypnosis. But all these healings will not be as necessary when mankind becomes and eats in balance with nature.

That concludes thoughts on healing.

This is your Wise Guide. You may now go unless you have questions.

Kathy, do you have a question?

Kathleen: No, I have no questions.

Have a good evening.

Mike's eyes are very tight . . . he is shaking . . . now he is calm.

Negative one came and went.

✿ GROWTH OF THE EVOLVING PERSONALITY

Thursday, December 31, 1981, Session 81

This is Seth II. Tonight, we will speak of the growth of the evolving personality.

When one is born into Earth's experience, one assumes the challenges of the human personality. Now the moment of birth, the place of birth, the circumstances of birth, all affect this emerging personality.

Each fragment or personality is working its own psychodrama with other personalities. Now the intent of this new personality is to work out commitments that were made before in past experiences as in between lives.

Let us say if in one life one assumes a personality of a female and lives out that life the next life they may choose to be a male and experience that life. One could say that every size, shape, color, religion, and sex of the human species is experienced.

Now in this experiencing certain learned personality traits based upon all these earthly multidimensional experiences are recorded within the soul's greater self. From this bank of experience and memory lessons are gathered and learned and personalities, new personalities, bring forth that data and accumulate new data.

Now to the degree that a human is in touch with their true self they can tap into this accumulated experience and knowledge. To the degree that the personality recognizes only the personality, there is wonder, confusion, frustration, that seemingly uncontrollable personality traits that manifest themselves early in young adult life. This will vary from culture to culture. One may be a young adult at 10 or 30.

Your psychologists appoint to the environment, to the upbringing, as reasons for behavior. The effect of environment and upbringing is important and can affect behavior but not in your generally recognized sense. It affects behavior because it generally puts constraints upon this new emerging personality, redefines it in their personal terms, and creates a structure by which this emerging personality becomes frustrated and confused. You have expressions regarding young children in their rebelling at a very young age say three or four.

Now when one enters through birth, the human body, one still has the memories of their greater nature and the freedom and creativity that existed there.

The human body and the human personality, if there was no greater soul and your life was truly your own existence would simply go through a nurturing period and run a life of trying to survive a particular culture, their whole life being one of constant survival.

This personality could be molded into anything as a young child. However, such is not the case and the personality does have a greater self or soul and does have various entities guiding the development of that personality. So, the personality both retains some feeling from the past with some experiences triggered by new experiences while still experiencing new situations in a lightly different way.

Now habit can be passed from experience to experience and indeed souls do tend to follow a line of development. If one were a winemaker in one life they might sell wine in another life, might make bottles or corks or may, of course, choose an entirely new line of work.

Personalities, therefore, carry forth both good and bad habits and in fact may choose to rid themselves of a habit that hinders the soul's growth.

Now indeed there is a challenge here. For it may go against a very old reinforced habit. The habit and circumstance and the choice chosen may be such that the personality places themselves in an experience environment that forces him to constantly confront the habit. Or may choose to set up a situation whereby they will not have to face that particular habit or problem. Eventually, all are faced through infinite time.

Now most personalities in your culture spend their time dealing with false fears but very real to the personality. This is a combination of some learned fears and some still upon the personality by the nature of family, social and political and religious structures. And I might add sexual taboos that seem to bridge all areas in your current culture. Now ancient cultures and past cultures readily accepted certain experiences that you fear and reject as personalities on Earth at this time. Those personalities many times choose not to enter the Earth's experience during a cultural experience such as yours. Some do to resolve a debt within themselves.

❀ NATURE OF PERSONALITY AND THE CHILD

Friday, January 1, 1982, Session 82
This is a Wise Wise One.

The nature of personality is such that it has from birth instincts for survival. Now when a personality is born, the soul is the closest to the child and yet by nature of free will the furthest from this newly emerging personality.

We must now speak of color in relationship to the human being since there is interference on the part of Michael's inner mind trying to assess and coordinate color, sound, frequency, with the personality.

This is a Wise Wise Wise One.

The soul being marked by color also manifests itself in color when incarnating in the form of a personality.

Mike is quiet, his eyes are shut, he is calm—I'm just waiting here—gap.

We will now continue with the emerging personality.

When the child is born, a new personality is born and charged with free will. The time, place, and circumstance of birth are generally chosen by the soul.

Now personality can be and has been referred to as the causal body when speaking of color within the auric field, but there is a mental body that represents the soul and the greater self. So, at the time of birth, like a child to a mother, a personality to the greater self is closest and yet furthest since like the child, it can only and generally only relate to sounds, vibrations, colors, touch, and feel warmth, and of course love, the seed of all creation in all life in each molecule, in each atom.

❀ DEVELOPMENT OF THE CHILD *(Same Session)*

Now the child's and personality's world is the world generally speaking of its mother. And during the first four to eight years of life there is an emerging personality based upon choice and guidance by both earthly structures and the intuitive, instinctive, and impulsive greater self, for there is an inner relation there.

A child will come forth with simplicity, honesty, and allowed to develop with guidance and firmness. The greater self will become more of the child at a sooner time. However, the nature of various cultures and societies has been to instill in the majority of children earthly philosophies primarily with an acceptance that there is something greater that is sometimes recognized as God's and sometimes simply as the elements.

Now, the nature of a child's upbringing may keep the child busy and cause inner conflict within the child based upon trying to reach their greater self and deal with the human experience.

The newly emerging personality will reflect learned principles from all the personalities within the greater self and not be aware of it. This accounts for the difference one sees in some children as opposed to another child or children along with earthly environmental upbringing. The seed of love accounts for the similarity between all personalities.

The seed of emotions accounts for the similarity of all personalities. The seed of the human body accounts for the similarity between all personalities that all, the above, are focused in the earthly experience.

Now given the nature of the development of the greater self and the purpose of the experience on Earth and justice and the circumstance, place, location of birth, the personality will show those similarities mentioned but may act differently and pursue different lines of development.

During the pursuit and living of the earthly experience, the inner conflicts that one feels are a combination of the inner conflicts of the personality, the greater self and the purpose, and the inner relationship with other personalities, and the justice of the earthly experience. The choice in how one progresses through the experience further determines the evolutionary development aspects of the greater self, i.e. the soul and the earthly personality. And each singular personality affects through their experiences, however, seemingly minutely all experience on Earth and in total consciousness.

For as difficult to fathom and understand, each thought put forth from a personality has a life, although not an eternal life of its own. It is picked up by other personalities sometimes as purposeful highly developmental, and sometimes as random thoughts, still sometimes as depressing un-developmental thoughts.

If personalities understand the importance of self-responsibility in guiding their destiny they would have a much smoother earthly experience. If personalities understood that self-responsibility of all personalities they would make VERY, VERY, valuable contributions to all personalities and to the Earth experience.

If personalities understood that all life, ALL is equal in the eyes of God, that the plant, the fish, the bird, the cow, all are loved equally and are equally valid in the eyes of God, the Earth experience would no longer be necessary. And new exciting experiences much more creative await this highly evolved personality which is part of a greater group of souls known as consciousness which is part of all that is which is God which cast forth all with love.

The end of dictation. This is your Wise Guide. Are there any questions this evening?

Mike: I have none.

Monday, January 4, 1982, Session 84
This is a Wise Wise One.

When a soul enters the human body it sometimes enters while a fetus just before birth and sometimes enters just after birth.

Now an energy form known as the causal body which is marked by color and consists of seven vibrating centers is the newly emerging personality. Having chosen the circumstance of birth, time, location, parents, etc. this personality while a child is more of the greater self while still being a free will personality. As a child is raised the physical aspects of the human body must develop naturally genetically with the order of the human species as a developmental guidepost.

Now while the human body is developing and growing through the process of birth, be young childhood, the emerging personality is developing and is generally listening to the greater self. But being a free will personality and thrust into an uncommon situation, that being Earth, it seeks to understand who it is and why it is here.

Now the physical body has natural reflexes and responses that can be alive without much energy or a minute fragment of the soul.

Understanding the purpose has much to do with the form and the focusing of the casual body in Earth's experience.

Now during the early years, a child generally knows his mother and father or guardians and is understanding and coping with the physical world and will pick up certain personality traits. However, a soul will bring with it learned habits from past lives that have been reinforced whether positive or negative and of course that is part of the purpose.

The fragment is one of many fragments of the same soul that may spend a reincarnation experience of 300 years, 100 years, or 50 years or any given amount of time.

Generally speaking with the various personalities that are focused within the experience a reincarnational time will run from 150 to 300 years.

Do you need a break?

Kathleen: No, I'm fine, thank you.

So, when the personality is inner facing with its Earth environment which is probably parents, guardians, or family, it is working with learned habits as well as and through parental or guardian direction of Earth's experience.

In dealing with the earthly guidance factor many personalities learn to become what their parents wish them to be or more accurately what their parents are. Caring forth structural beliefs, religious beliefs, earthly beliefs, that their parents have taught them. This is further reinforced by various teachers in development through the childhood and teenage years. This general statement applies to ancient times, modern times, all times, all cultures, though the time frames may be slightly different from culture to culture.

This also causes conflict within the individual personality where within themselves they feel compelled to pursue a line of development that may not be consistent with earthly teachings be it positive or negative.

Each personality on your Earth has been, is, and will be subject to those conditions. Understanding that if mass consciousness decided to adopt a policy that allowed each to self-create with gentle guidance and love as opposed to judgment, and positive as opposed to negative reinforcement, wars would disappear for the most part, creativity would blossom and life on Earth would be greatly significantly less stressful, more happy, and a positive development for each and all of the human species.

If it were to be that all species of life worked to love all life, Earth would be a paradise.

That concludes dictations. Are there any questions?

Mike: No questions.

Then I bid you good evening and love to all.

This is your Wise Guide are there any general questions?

Mike: I have none.

Have a good evening.

✿ WHAT IT MEANS TO "WANT"

Friday, January 15, 1982, Session 92

This is a Wise One. We will discuss wanting.

A want is a desire, a need, something to fulfill an individual personality on Earth. Now there are many wants and needs that the human personality, depending upon the experience, a want or a need can be physical, can be a material, or can be a mental. Now in your history, you humans focused on Earth at this time are aware of many wants have been redefined according to man. In so doing they chose a method of instilling fear or guilt within the human being for wanting or desiring.

If a man desired another man physically there was much fear and guilt instilled depending upon all mankind about such an action. If a man desired a woman it is generally okay if a woman desired a man there again men instilled fear into women's hearts. If a man or woman desired material objects there was guilt associated with that, also. Now where a want or a need harms no one else then one on Earth has lost nothing in the experience. If a want or a need is out of love given then there is benefit to the experience on Earth. Now with all the laws, traditions, structures man has built for himself, it is a sad state of affairs when men or women are told not to want or desire for there is nothing wrong with wanting and desiring given it doesn't hurt another life form.

Wanting is natural and we stress that here this evening so that you may know that there is nothing wrong with that emotion or for that matter any emotion.

Mike is sleeping. He is now awake. That was quick.

This is your Wise Guide. When one wants one should go with one's natural instinct and it should lead one to the correct choice. Now that simple sentence says much more than you know.

We will conclude sessions and answer any questions that you might have.

Kathleen: I have no questions.

Then have a good evening.

FOR THOSE SEEKING LOVE AND UNDERSTANDING

January 31, 1982, Session 105

This is one who is seeking love and understanding.

Before one enters a human experience, one makes certain commitments, for when one enters one develops an emerging personality. This personality has free will and can pursue any path that it so desires. Now enlightened souls understand that through love and understanding of how love functions within Earth's dimension can reach this emerging personality and guide it.

The emerging personality is affected by soul experience and soul understanding and is indeed affected by Earth's experience and Earth's understanding.

Therefore, most exist a conflict, an inner conflict that is constantly questioning what one sees and what one hears. That inner voice when followed will lead one to an understanding of one's inner being and development. Those who try and stifle that inner voice by the nature of free will can do so. But since the Earth's living is such a minor part of infinite love within the confines of one lifetime it impedes the soul's progress and stifles the development of a human personality.

Each personality brings with it all of its experience though it is rare to have all experience recalled and a good thing, too.

What is important, what is remembered about God and love's guidance. Through justice and seeking all other thoughts finally come to rest, and those not in concert with love, fade away within the soul never to be heard of again. The personality that is forced into human situations and through no intent is fine. The personality who realizes and understands that it is not consistent with love to infringe upon another's free will without their consent to do something that is harmful to their progress without their consent shall choose to have the same thing done to them through the principle of justice and like attracts like.

Martin Luther King was a wise person. And is a good example of what we have spoken of. He is on a good path toward love and God. He said I have a dream and what he envisioned is a dream for him that will come true.

No bullet or misdeed can stop a loving nature, it, of course, is reborn, but even within the human experience lives one within each for love shared grows.

PERSONALITY AND SOUL IN THE BODY

Thursday, February 11, 1982, Session 114
I Am That I Am.

We will speak of consciousness, thought physical being. Consciousness is the creative mind and is what humans refer to as the soul.

When thought is projected within the order of the human it, as far as personality goes, does not manifest within the child until just before or just after birth. Until then the fetus is developing as a physical form and is of a different order. The human body itself and what makes up the human body cells, atoms, etc., is part of a different order. The human personality uses the human body for a house. Now, that order which makes up the human body is of the same soul. It through physic connections unknown to the soul's personality except in highly elevated situations is somewhat of a mystery.

The soul is the mind and personality of the human body and it focuses within seven centers marked by color creating an aura within the human.

The personality and the human body experience together that which they have agreed upon. The personality develops within the framework of humanities structures, laws, and belief and yet is indeed linked to its greater self. And has guides not focused in this experiential reality, guides that are assigned and follow these souls and fragment personalities throughout their evolutionary process until they have found God and themselves.

The body responds to the thinking and attitude within the personality. The soul responds to its understanding of love and justice. And the newly emerging personality responds to all about it and within it for it is the experience, the doing. When love exists and is understood on the soul mind then the efficiencies within the body which are chosen do not limit that mind.

Now the personality is linked to every element within the universe in some manner or form. The most important understanding the personality can have is one of loving all, give justly from the heart or mind, and treat all as you would want to be treated.

The personality continues to exist forever and in almost all cases finds its way back to its greater self in a short period of time but loses none of its free will and gains understanding. Now when the fragment is projected it is and has as a part of it all soul memories and understands and its probable future on a psychic level. Many people recognize this and call it déjà vu, extrasensory perception, prophesying, etc.

Thursday, March 11, 1982, Session 134
This is a Wise One.

The soul chooses as a method of finding more understanding and experience. The soul learns and knows intuitively that anything that it projects or creates has within it inherent free will.

The personality when it returns to a non-experiential life and returns back to its normal state if less evolved will assume itself to be that one personality. When more evolved will understand itself to be many personalities.

The personalities whether knowing they belong to the soul that created them or not, exist independently and yet as a part of the soul linked to the soul by love, free will and thought, justice and order. The personality, all portions of the souls, as all souls, understands that there is more and greater learning.

A personality fragment can and does split off from its greater self to perform a mission. The personality will return to its greater self for rest, meditation, and peace at last understanding who it truly is. And yet still remains as vibrant and creatively oriented more so as a matter of fact as it always has and always will be. Souls create as they feel the need to create (lies) within the experience for the soul's betterment. For a newly created personality is based upon the souls understanding a free form experiment allowing a personality to develop and learn within a given experience.

The more personalities that are reunited with the soul the more learned the soul is and generally speaking the more careful the soul is in choosing experience. This analogy would hold true for the soul and God or all that is. Like God and I Am the greater soul is always intricately connected to a greater self.

The new personality learning and developing with a goal and learning objective can choose on its own based upon its free will to follow any pursuit that it wishes. Just as a child can choose to run away from its parents or to try and do what it pleases without accepting or looking to guidance from guardians or loved ones. The soul is always there within for any newly experiencing personality.

Your soul no matter where you go as a personality is connected through electrical impulse and is focused through sound and color.

When a soul looks within there is some wonder at what is happening about the soul or personality, but deep within there usually comes forth some answers or guidance. The evolving personality will, by looking within or by pursuing God's laws, gain greater knowledge and understanding of its true nature. The personality could, without any input, but just existing and surviving, know and express an experience, only in its immediate surroundings.

The personality pursuing experience upon its own has inherently within it, love, free will, and thought. And those elements are within everything created forever. When the personality tries to function against these infinite realities and truths it creates just experience. Within all exist God and there lies the interrelation between all and within the greater self.

Those truths are indeed operational principles not just for peace and happiness but for existence itself. So, to understand how and why one comes to realize its true nature and comes to realize truth is to merely understand those principles of thought, love, and free will. As it relates to the personality the greater self and all for it forms all, is all, and forever will be all. It is the I Am, the God, the being of all. It exists within all.

Whether or not a personality or element understands those basic truths they will continue to exist for it is at the core of all elements beginnings, endings, and forever mores. Through experience, any experience, one runs smack up against those truths. And comes to realize and pursue and exist forever and ever those wisdoms and truths that are themselves thought, love, free will.

And one element does not shrink, diminish, or becomes less by understanding truth but grows infinitely multidimensionally and joyously, happily, peacefully.

When one tries to change those truths then the paradoxical portion of justice comes into play. For what is given intentionally and freely from within is returned. When the wisest thought of loving all was expressed in the term 'do unto others as you would have them do unto you' the extension of that statement is that they are you. For all are a part and an operational portion of God.

We will conclude for this evening.

Friday, September 3, 1982, Session 231
The soul will always receive what it has planned. The soul does focus and create a freely evolving personality. The personality we refer to is the human personality. It evolves based upon current human experience which has many factors. That statement just refers to the human personality. The human personality was essentially emotional and intellectual in mind and nature. The emotions are interrelated to the human body and to the thinking process and to energy levels and to those about them. The soul plants thoughts that the human personality deals with rejecting or accepting and actioning. The soul does not have an emotional nature but a mental nature. Love in its purest form is not emotional. Love in its pure form is operational. When a soul is planting thoughts for the human personality the human personality will take those thoughts and apply them as best the human personality understands.

Now the human personality is a part of the soul and the soul is a part of God and therefore, the human personality is a part of God as all energy forms are. Now, when the soul is evolving it is evolving through creating and through experience. The creation is the human personality, the experience is the human personality. Of course, the soul focuses within other experiences and order.

Now when the soul is not focused within an experience the soul is assimilating the mind processes more or less like a dream state with a semi-rest or meditative state. The soul when focused within a reality such as the human personality is connected to God and the degree of the soul is evolved will allow the human personality to find God, also. For the human personality has a soul as a part of it and yet can feel separated or try to separate through emotions.

But it is not truly separated for each as a rest period. The human personality sleeps and returns through energy and elec-tromagnetic thought impulses to communicate with the soul or portions of the soul. Through evolution, many have attributed and interpreted God as at the greater self, as something greater with more power, with more wisdom and knowledge and in one general manner of speaking this can be true. God the creator of all, the creator of all evolutionary Gods, is mind being thought as well as is manifested by all that is and has true pure absolute giving love. Asking nothing in return, understanding that all that is given is returned in the manner in which it is given.

Because God exists in all as part of evolution and truth, all can find and touch God by being God-like and by practicing God like truths.

We will conclude for this evening.

✿ THE HUMAN PERSONALITY

Notebook #42, Page 5
The human personality is free-willed and contained in and about the body. The human personality functions about the body as aura and free will thought and in the body as energy, centers that vibrate and send forth electrochemical responses throughout the body and about the body.

The relationship does not continue upon the death of the body and at times for some human personalities, they for a while are not aware of the break in the relationship.

The human personality conveys then with the soul to greater and lesser degrees. The human personality can remain as a completely evolving unit for as long as it wishes and can create many realities to gain understanding.

However, the personality cannot focus as the same exact personality into another physical existence in the human body. The personality for that must make some contact with a greater self and work with its soul-self, although it may know (the human personality) be aware that they are one. They just know that it is someone who is helping them.

Now the human personality is evolving at the time of birth without the help of the soul. The soul will not normally enter the human role and work with the personality until the child reaches the age of reason.

This is normally at the age of approximately seven. Seven is somewhat of an acceptable number in the evolvement of the soul and the universe.

The human personality relates to the body through various energy centers in the body normally respond to physical realities known to it.

Now the thinking personality can be controlled or driven by these energy centers that relate to physical and natural environment and make or drive the personality.

This type of personality will respond to its environment not knowing that it has the power to, through the mind, change those circumstances.

The human personality in most situations is taught and guided by other human personalities and will respond in a human personality way based upon what they have been taught. However, the personality as it goes through life and thinks and reasons will ask questions, and when those questions do not find acceptable answers, the human personality will begin the reach within to greater and lesser degrees. The soul will send forth mind responses and images and thoughts and make a connection with the human personality to greater and lesser degrees at this time.

Now much contact is made in the sleep and dream state when the body is at rest and the energy centers in the body are at rest, and the personality, which is eternal, is not at rest but is learning, experiencing, and creating, most free time for most human personalities. The human personality incidentally orders that it remember all its experiences for as long as they are valid and necessary to evolutionary growth.

The human personality when dreaming or meditating will get some contact with greater realities. This is all a part of the evolutionary process. The soul is going through a like process and remembers through the human personality all that it needs to evolve effectively.

This, of course, applies to all portions, the soul, even those functioning in other realities.

The soul has the same evolving relationship with God. The intent is to evolve to a Godlike co-creating state, is God's will, God's love.

THOUGHT CENTERS

Friday, July 2, 1982, Session 197
This is a Wise One.

When one thinks, there is a giving and receiving of electrical impulses and energy mass. This occurs about and in the body. The body relates and reacts and functions by process of the human mind when speaking of the human being. This process is indeed centered in seven focal or energy points of the body that are directly connected to the thought process of the soul. These seven centers each function independently of the human body and yet are connected to it through evolutionary purpose.

Each center will send off vibrations and frequencies that will affect to some degree or another all centers of the body. For instance, the center known as the groin sends off electrical impulses to the gonads in the male and the ovaries in the female. It also sends off impulses to the general female organs or male organs that might arouse or will affect that area. The impulse travels to the brain which centers the mind portion of the human personality but not the soul or greater soul for the human personality in total is freely evolving.

Other centers correspond to the emotional nature of mankind and send electrical impulses through the body to the specifically defined areas of the body. The type of thought and quality of thought determines the electrical magnetical or electrical chemical energy in and about the body.

Now it is possible for a human to not have one of these centers to operate and respond to. The centers are the mechanics of what makes the physical body movement and are projected by the soul evolving through experience.

Each of these centers relates directly to the human mind and the human body, blood, muscles, corpuscles, bone, and all the physicalness that relates to these centers. The actual physical body is not connected to the soul. For the human body is part of an order of development that for a general statement could be considered a prop in a play for the play takes place in the mind and moves about in props as that play evolves.

Substitute the part of the play for life and you will begin to understand. Now, these centers each can and generally do contain different vibrational levels and yet are still projected by the evolving soul and are still under the laws of love guided by the human mind.

As a soul evolves and projects each center increases and decreases and vibrational energy, justly so, meaning that one can have a sexual center apart from an anger center which is in the abdominal region or a fear center which is in the region of the chest that can react from messages sent from the mind and cause physical response in the body.

Each center also interrelates. Each center puts forth energy marked by color. The colors, of course, can be different and are in reflected imagery. Some centers can seemingly dominate the physical body if the human mind allows it or chooses it. All centers relate to the quality of one's thought. When a soul is in harmony each center vibrates more harmoniously. It is possible for a group of souls that form an entity to create change, the vibrational frequency and energy and aura of the human body by focusing and adding or supplanting various centers. This to be done requires a high level of vibrational understanding and achievement. This is very, very, very, rarely done. In almost every conceivable case there have been exchanges made of souls within the human body. It is done in the crown area leaving the personalities or those gravity centers or energy centers intact. In summary, the human personality more than likely remains and evolves with another at the helm, so to speak. This is also done by highly evolved souls.

In referring to fear centers and anger centers they also contain many other emotions. Quality of thought will determine the harmony by which all centers work together or the degree by which one center will override another center. Now there is also the human body that is connected to all these centers through sensory perception. Each species develops and or has developed certain sensory perceptions by which to exist on Earth.

Now just as the soul can ignore the validity of the greater soul-self or even a God and perceives itself a God in itself so too can the mind ignore a greater soul-self and perceive itself as the total being, so too the center poorly developed can separately exert control on other's centers in terms of biochemical reactions, so too can the body exert upon the centers.

Certain needs but all relate to the human evolving mind or to the soul fragment or soul itself depending upon the evolutionary place of the soul and depending upon just endeavors.

For example, the human mind can reject or accept the various diseases that mankind invents. The human mind can cure or be cured by the thought process. This is not to say that it is the only method of curing and that medicine is not valuable for it is to the human species as long as it is believed to be so.

When one leaves one will no longer require medicine, there is no pain other than self-inflicted pain by the evolving soul. The body sends messages to the centers and relates pleasure and pain. The mind can accept or reject those senses or if the body is not in harmony can distort those senses.

The intensity of the thought or message sent to a center determines the effect of all centers and mentalness. The soul then is or rather has been told to have many different bodies.

One can have a need or symptom treated be it of a physical nature or a mental nature and if the mind accepts the validity of treatment then healing occurs. The best treatment is evolving internal problems then the symptoms drop and fade away.

We will conclude the session by saying, what you find beings recognize and love is the highest quality thought that self-love does not send messages to all centers but just to the center of being concerned. A love given sends messages to all centers simultaneously and, of course, each center in any situation sends out its message to the body and the body sends out its message to the physical world.

There are some who visually see colors, some who sense, and some who smell the change. For the body sends forth many vibrations by the method just discussed.

Have a good evening and there is one here who will now speak to your wife.

I Am the Love that shines forth through all. There are many here; many working for this purpose speaking through many on Earth. We wish to say we are pleased with you, wise woman.

Mike took my hand to draw. I drew a face similar to the one on the cover.

✿ THE CONTRAST: BAD PEOPLE AND BAD DEEDS

Saturday, August 21, 1982, Session 222
This is a Wise One.

The soul remembers all; within the soul and about the soul is every thought. The soul remembers all but those memories drop away and become vague, very vague, remembrances. Those memories can be brought back when jogged by circumstance or event. A human personality carries within it a greater self that is the soul.

Almost without exception human personalities while upon Earth come in contact with their greater self. Most of the contact is through the dream state. The human personality sends thought impulses as it thinks, and the soul personality sends forth thought impulses as it thinks. Those thoughts are directed to the evolving personality and to other realities. The human personality remembers from dreams some soul thoughts that within the human world are many times referred to as subconscious thoughts. However, most humans now treat the thoughts as being entirely related to human endeavor and take those thoughts and interpret them, relating them to the human endeavor. Where those thoughts do not fit in with conventional feelings of the time the thinker is perceived as an outcast and labeled with various outcast labels.

Now, why does a human suddenly without any seeming reason commit violent acts? Why does a human suddenly without any seeming reason do something very contradictory to their nature? Why does a human destroy without seeming conscious? Those questions cannot be fully dealt with within the framework of human endeavor, or, can they be fully dealt within the framework of soul endeavor.

However, acts out of the norm can be classified as unfulfillment.

Now, symptoms of unfulfillment can be violence, greed, lust, anger, any number of reactions or actions. Now the unfulfillment quite simply is a lack of understanding of the basic self.

Now fulfillment takes many paths and steps so one may become involved in an unacceptable act believing they will be fulfilled. One can treat and does treat these human individuals according to currently accepted practices which vary from culture to culture and time to time within the realm of Earth's experience.

In learning to become fulfilled many, most, work within structured frameworks. Accepting those rules and regulations rather than stretching for greater fulfillment, of course, the soul accepts this and even plans it before a life experience begins. Understanding that frameworks offer some order to an evolving personality and having learned that serving "many Masters" creates much confusion.

The outcast who may become infamous in Earth's history is one who lacks discipline when those acts are so irrational.

Now, these individuals outwardly exhibit seeming discipline, but their vision and scope is narrow which limits and confines their activities and always brings about defeat for their purposes.

Occasionally you will find one who gains much power and rises to lead many. This does not change the nature of that individual, they still are unfulfilled and undisciplined internally. Now we have chosen the word unfulfilled because it has a very broad-based application, it relates directly to self-love. There are many symptoms to self-love and those are generally treated. There are many ways of treating those symptoms, those guilts, fears, insecurities. What is forgotten in time and perspective is the purpose of evolution and the truth of God. Not the God of fear who punishes, but God of Love who has bestowed upon each free will, and upon each the freedom to create, and the promise that they will get what they give.

When one is treating unfulfillment, any step to help is a step in the right and correct direction, eventually.

Now we are speaking of an individual, any individual, and leaving behind or leaving out for the moment a history of mankind, a history of a culture, we are speaking to that individual.

Evolution is for the purpose of learning and understanding how to think and create in a disciplined manner following the principles of love and following the framework of God's will. In the end, the infinite end, that is the broadest framework that exists for it transcends all, is a part of all, and is in all. And for the moment we are leaving out the just evolution of the individual meaning their particular problems they may be facing and created and have been created by them. And they are facing them or experiencing them to understand themselves.

For the moment we concentrate just upon the individual and start at their beingness. There are many techniques and applications to reach and touch one's beingness for each look and finds it in a uniquely free will individual manner or it finds them.

Now, most define love as strictly feeling or emotion fixed within their personal world. All without exception, your worst and your best, by our definition upon Earth know that they have love within them. To treat any, including the outcasts that we have described, based upon the principles of love, to treat now in time if it is 8:02 A.M. in the morning and you are having a conversation with your outcast, our common ground is now. What you both have in common within you is love. Some, of course, are more understanding and wiser.

Now, we understand the conflict upon Earth when one says to forgive and yet observes somebody committing perhaps a terrible act. We say this, each no matter what they have done is possessed of love and each will receive in full measure in one manner or another, fully what they have created no matter if you have forgiven them or not. To judge another will bring about the same judgment to you. We understand the difficulty in not judging a killer, a rapist, a person of violence, and not applying some revenge or restitution by judging their acts immoral.

We further understand the conflict between free will misused and freedom. And yet we say that forgiveness is divine. We understand thought, and are aware thought evolution requires order and law and discipline. The law of God must be read carefully for there are many wise truths behind each law.

Where lies from the human perspective and justice in killing, murder, rape, and various crimes? Where lies the discipline that allows it to exist? What prevents one from applying God's laws to a so-called outcast and having that outcast take advantage? We say this, treat each as you would wish to be treated. And Jesus Christ said 'render unto Caesar what is Caesars' simply stated if a soul chooses to work within a framework or a fraction of a soul chooses to work in a framework they understand the conditions and laws in that framework. They understand in one sense or another the rewards for their actions.

The fact is simple, each, each, evolving element of God is still working out the difference between self-love and love of the self. For one should not feel fear in feeling good about the self and will feel good about the self. Understand that each is possessed of love and can be reached through love.

Practice that and new enlightenment will begin, though not without a battle. Implement your laws but know this, you will receive what you give. That is not to strike fear in the hearts of evolving souls, for God measures intentions and wishes, you do what is in your heart.

Render unto your laws, accept what you cannot change and change what you cannot accept. But life upon Earth, evolution upon Earth, or within the realm of the soul, the multidimensional soul, is now. For fulfillment in the most continuing basis understand that—that comes by walking in God's love, not human love.

And here we present God's love. Love all. When you have a love given you have a love received. When you have a love held closely you have a love held closely. When you judge, judge wisely for you will be judged likewise. Love for the endeavor and receive rewards manifold. Love for the reward and you will receive the reward. Forgive and be forgiven. Mercy and have mercy. Create for all and that what you create will be returned by all. Create for few and that which you create will be returned by few. Create for the self and there is no one to return it, but the self.

Love the smallest and the greatest equally. Give from your heart, mind, and soul, and you will receive many blessings. Give from your ego and you will receive that which mankind gives. Run from fear and it grows. Run to fear and it diminishes and finally disappears. Run from love and it diminishes but will never disappear. Run to love and it grows.

Each human as each element is a part of God. Each human has a greater soul-self and each soul-self ascends to God. Love the justice in your heart for the justice in your heart you will have. Do what you do to learn, avoid what you avoid having learned and understood its nonbeneficial nature. Do what you avoid, not out of fear, out to learn. Treat each as you wish to be treated and you will evolve wisely.

To have is to not understand. To lose what you have is to not understand and yet you shall have both of these and understand, that is finding peace and God. Each thinks. Each creates. Each freely thinks. Each love. Each chooses. Each accepts what you have chosen and learn by it and go and grow. Each will find God. And through the grace of God each can find God at any moment that they so will it. And peace will come.

When you walk in God's will, you walk in true free will. When you walk in your will, tread wisely for there are many paths within the self. God is all. God is love. God is thought. All think. Freely. Individually. Help is love. Finding comes from within. When one chooses to win for the self, one chooses a temporary false victory. When one chooses to win for God, one gains an infinite victory.

Wise one we will spend a few minutes alone now.

🏵 PERSONALITY, SOUL, AND SPIRIT

Sunday, September 26, 1982, Session 242
This is a Wise One.

The personality and the soul and the spirit will evolve together. The personality evolves freely, the soul evolves freely, the spirit evolves freely. All are connected to that which is truth. Within the human endeavor, the human personality is what is referred to as the personality that which manifests itself as the creative element and the creator of the personality is the soul. That which manifest itself as the higher realms of the soul which contain orders also is the spirit. That which binds all is the truth and the truth is God.

When the personality is focused upon Earth there are some mechanisms that can only be released through some electrical impulses that open up certain channels between the personality and the soul. Need is one, another is hope, and there is love. Recognizing the difference, the personality and the soul from an objective point of view is basic. The personality is focused within time, place, and events. The personality if it were a singular unit would relate and respond based upon time, place, and events. Summed up, as the personality's environmental understanding, the world, of course, would have long since been destroyed for there have been times when the time, place, and events were essentially survival, one against another where fear ruled almost entirely. Those times will come again and pass again. The souls who are focusing within that time, place, and event sequence, are not as learned. However, there are always some that rise beyond the time, place, and events sequence and reach within and find a greater soul self. In which situation, the soul self and the personality act somewhat together to greater or lesser degrees.

Spirituality is then greater elements of the soul that must be and is reached and can speak of higher realms yet. Many great religions and minor religions have been created out of perception of an interpretation of spirituality, soulness, and personality.

The spiritual world has various levels and elements that work within the evolutionary levels of the soul to bring greater awareness of truth. They are teachers, they are guides, some have evolved through the Earth's plain, some have not incarnated within the Earth's sphere, and some have not incarnated at all.

But all will in one system or another. Spirituality can be thought of as souls evolving on higher plains learning on higher levels how to be co-creators of learning on alternative levels.

It is necessary and appropriate to break these, shall we say developmental fields, into these particular subsections. Of course, there are many more sections, subsections, and orders, but to speak of these is to speak of something that the human personality can relate to in one matter or other.

The human personality knows that it is focused in this world. Many know that they have a soul-self and believe in for the most part a God or a supreme being.

Tuesday, November 2, 1982, Session 261
Without stating specific detail, we have stated the general description of the multidimensional thought creative process that is the soul, entering a system focusing and separating into all orders within an evolving system. Each order possessed of individual soul elements that have thought, love, and free will as a part of their being and a total of their being. Each is created and returns to the creator.

Each fragment is a part of a whole. When the soul leaves the evolving system as a more fully understanding being, the soul advances on to other creative endeavors being more fully intoned with God. Each experience that the soul has experienced remains as a part of the soul as a memory of the soul.

Using the analogy of the human personality.

The human personality is created by the conditions in which it enters and is affected by those elements that it wishes to be affected by or has been taught to be affected by. The human personality assumes personality traits. The human personality goes through an ebb and flow cycle. The flow is the dream, the ebb is the experience, though the personality perceives it in the reverse. The human personality is a being of its own and functions as that being until it, on its own terms, comes to the realization that it is more than a singular adversely alone being. At which time it recognizes that it is not against a world or other personalities and need not defend itself but recognizes that it is part of a greater soul-self. That if left alone could only create within the environment that it knows.

The greater soul has explored all environments or will explore all environments through the creation of personalities. There is an absolute interrelation between the personality and the soul because the soul creates the personality. The personality when left predominately alone will defend its existence. The personality's thoughts and speech in almost all situations are stories about themselves and their thoughts being projected out to others for the diversification of the personality. The personality recognizes that it has free will and can do what it wishes to greater and lesser degrees. Some personalities continue on their own for a long time in human terms looking to continue an existence within a human body as themselves.

The personality is made up of thought, will, and love. The thought is for survival on its own, the will attempts to implement this, and the love is what it really searches for. However hard an element of God might try is never alone, cannot exist alone, and there are inner relationships with all. The personality that continues after leaving the physical body to attempt a physical life again, cannot create another being. Within the human body are seven energy centers that have an inner relationship with the soul, the experience, and God.

We will conclude for this evening.

THE HOLY TRINITY FORMS

Notebook #24, Page 15
This is a Wise One.

The nature of the personality is such that they, the personality, will seek those earthly pursuits that best mean for survival on Earth. Left alone the personality would attach itself to earthly pursuits and follow only earthly instincts. The personality, of course, would not be without the soul for the personality is a part of the soul, as the soul is a part of the personality. However, the human has a casual body—which is the personality, a mental body—which is the soul, and a spiritual body—which is the thought of love, is the element known as God. When first on Earth, the personality is knowing of the soul or the greater self and is seeking, in some cases to understand that greater self just as the soul in some cases is seeking to understand its greater consciousness, that being the spiritual, thought, love, God body of which all come from and are a part of these form the Holy Trinity.

This is a Wise One. Read those words again for they are very true and simple and wise words.

The personality, the soul, the spiritual body form the Holy Trinity that has been mentioned.

The Father, the Son, the Holy Ghost.

The soul, the personality, the spiritual being, that is the seed of all.

These are the Trinity, the Holy Trinity.

❀ THE MANY BODIES THAT MAKE UP THE HUMAN

Notebook #29, Page 14

This is a Wise One.

The nature of the physical human can indeed be different from the mental human. There are many bodies that go to make up the human. They are physical, personality, mental, consciousness, God or spiritual body.

Now with certain religions and structures, they break it down slightly differently as they do levels of development and understanding.

The physical body is that which genetically develops according to conditions of humanity and human or mankind needs it. That required more strength or more color or different sexual parts than it was so genetically developed. Physical attractiveness between adults does not truly occur. There is a nice look but that is as far as it actually goes. The attraction is of the etheric body or the consciousness body or the mental body or the soul body or God body.

Now the God body or soul body contains all bodies as a part of its individual whole. All bodies are not forged with free will, that which is forged with free will is all but the physical body. All other bodies are said to be separate, but they are no more separate than the ear is from the physical body. When on incarnates the physical body is already essentially developed or the genetic program is already programmed. The personality or what is also referred to as the astral body is somewhat programmed based upon lines of planned development but forged with free will and is able to freely choose although there are strong pulls based upon justice that do affect this personality. The color of the personality is reflected initially as white at birth and is colored differently as other bodies

are integrated into this personality body. The mental consciousness and soul bodies are used to describe various activities and
directions and structures used to total soul evolvement or development. The levels, plains, or bodies are merely the soul finding
its true nature which is always greater than it knows or thinks.

On the evolutionary cycle, the soul becomes more integrated
into multidimensional directions exploring mental, exploring
emotional, and creating within each multidimensional experience. This evolutionary process is also similar for other orders
and a true soul may take eons of time to become aware of its true
self and still be a co-creator with God. The order of development is
important for those within those orders and important to a wholly
unique experience, like the Earth experience. That all order is
interrelated in a shared reality both as unique component parts
of the whole but as interrelated parts of its own unique whole.

❁ THE GREATER SELF

Notebook #37, Page 8
This is a Wise One.

The complexity of the personality can be simplified when one
accepts that within lies a Greater Self who has experienced before.
The Greater Self knows far more than the personality can learn in
one life, however, what the personality learns in life is important
to that life and will be remembered in other lives.

JESUS SPEAKS

Godly souls are souls who
volunteer themselves to
speak the word of All.

A final understanding of love's truth
lies within each person's understanding
on Earth and each soul's understanding wherever.

CHAPTER 7

JESUS SPEAKS

Jesus came forth many times to speak. Jesus spoke of love, soul, the light of truth and greater consciousness. The chapter begins with a definition of Godly souls; Jesus is an example of a Godly soul. Godly Souls—enlightened souls—who come into existence to share the Word of God. A message, or rather, a reminder, that love is the seed of all that God has created. The intentional presence of these Godly Souls is crucial to mankind's understanding of God and God's laws, and the selfless power of Jesus' purpose and crucifixion for the benefit of mankind. Jesus reminds us to seek not outside ourselves, but to look within and ask for guidance; answers will be given.

Jesus also speaks on the soul consciousness and how molecules and atoms create our shared universe and have a greater self. He speaks of understanding that there is a supreme order and thought that connects all. Jesus makes an analogy of life as a very good movie, where one plays various roles and without each role, the movie could not exist or be of quality. He connects that thought with a comparative reference to God.

So, come sit with us.
These messages are meant for you.

(DICTATION BEGINS)

✿ GODLY SOULS

Tuesday, November 24, 1981, Session 57
Mike is writing very slowly.

This is a Godly Soul.

Love is the Truth.

Godly souls are souls who volunteer themselves to speak the word of All. Each civilization has a few such souls, who out of a great understanding of love, lead mankind and other experiential endeavors to God's laws of creation. Jesus is such a soul. Lao Tzu is such a soul. Confucius is such a soul. There are a few that speak the Word.

✿ JESUS SPEAKS ON CREATION

Wednesday, January 13, 1982, Session 91
This Is Jesus.

You have heard from a wise, very wise soul. And what has been spoken of is what is understood by this very wise soul.

I Am That I Am forged all orders with free will, but all orders are interrelated through love, and all orders on the creative level, for all orders do create, and all orders do think, and all orders do ascend to an elevated level, so to speak, and all orders become one when with the true understanding of love and the nature of love and thought and truth and God and all that is. The smallest atoms that create your universe have a consciousness of their own, but different order, but a different self-responsibility so to speak, without the same degree of energy, for it is not required in their system—and yet a greater degree of understanding and freedom than what man knows as the soul consciousness. For as fragments, create the Earth's experience and yet have a greater self, so too, molecules and atoms create your universe and have a greater self. And with God the supreme understanding, the creator of all; all forms of consciousness exist equally.

Understanding that there is a supreme order that connects all, and that is All. A supreme thought that connects all, and that is All. That is love and anything created by the nature of God is and forever maintains consciousness and free will and it grows in love and understanding and creates.

Imagine a very good movie that can make you laugh, make you feel good, just take you away, enjoyable. And imagine that you are the producer, director, and can be an actor at any time and can be anything within that play, that movie, and get the full enjoyment of giving and expressing and loving. Without a producer, there is no movie. Without a director, there would not be the same quality movie. Without actors, stagehands, etc., in order for the movie to continue the experience, all must contribute. Those that contribute out of love and desire for all gain and are recognized that way by all viewing. God is the viewer, the creator, the participant, God is All. Each participant or element has a part that is of equal importance to sustain creation. For this evening that is as close to analogy as I can come.

Each minute element of a person's body is giving out of love to sustain that body. There are orders within orders within the human body, within the Earth, animals, plants, that come together to create and enjoy the experience of Earth and to learn. Yes, there is an alliance between various orders that seem to experience together. Even one's same heart might have been the same heart within another human experience, coming together again to participate together. The giving of love is more beautiful than one can imagine or dream of. The understanding of love, the fulfillment of love, the freedom of love.

There are infinite, infinite experiences in God's thoughts.

And God is truly within each and is truly a part of each. Each act of giving from the heart brings one closer to understanding.

I will give blessings now to those in this room and this house for the love of all.

Good night wise ones.

This is your Wise Guide. Are there any questions?

Mike: I have none.

Have a good evening and love to you all.

✿ JESUS SPEAKS ON LOVE

Notebook #22, Page 3

I am Jesus. I will speak of Love.

Love is the thought of which the soul was created. Love is the thought by which all was created. Love is service to all life with an understanding that all life is part of each form. Love is the service of love, for the creator of all.

Love is the service for the understanding that all are created equally in the eyes of God.

Love is order in that out of this creation of individually forged free will consciousness form all are separate but a part of shared reality.

Love is the responsibility that each creates through attitude a learned reality and that attitude determines that reality.

Love is the knowledge that error is human. Love is the understanding that error in the pursuit of love is just and the love in the pursuit of error is not just.

Love is the requirement of justice for all consciousness.

Love is the belief in a greater force of good.

Love is responsibility to the greater self without greater self-denial.

Love is a service of wanting to serve God.

In the year "O" on Earth, love was upon Earth in the beauty through which the order of the plant world manifested. Plant reality. Giving to all and asking nothing in return and receiving thereby everything. The plant world on Earth is one of governing factors. Those factors being metamorphosis, photosynthesis, justice and love, each contributing as a separate factor and being a part of the greater factor.

The plants are a homogenous group by nature. When that is not the case it is man's recreating a plant environment. Plants understand and accept this as a part of their giving through love their beauty a substance to life on Earth. All are part of the shared reality and have an equal place in it. It takes away nothing from the forged free will upon the soul. The greatest service of free will is to understand that we are all a part of a shared reality forever and will contribute and receive forever. That the love of all is the seed of true consciousness.

The meaning of giving is what one receives. When one gives from the heart, one receives in the heart. When one justly gives one receives just gifts. When one openly gives one receives grandly. When one gives, one understands the meaning of receiving. When one understands the meaning of receiving, then one justly gives openly from the heart. When one understands the meaning of giving, then one openly receives grand and just gifts from the heart. To give is to receive. To receive is to give. They are the same.

✿ LOVE'S TRUTH

January 31, 1982, Session 105
This is Jesus.

A final understanding of love's truth lies within each person's understanding of Earth and each soul's understanding wherever. For through free will one travels many paths in pursuit of truth. When those about you are not in agreement with what you know, then look within and ask for guidance, it is there. Each soul, each person on Earth, understands this at the core of its being.

✿ UNDERSTANDING ONE'S SELF

Tuesday, January 12, 1982, Session 90
This is Jesus. I will speak of understanding one's self.

The personality and soul are both born into the physical world to evolve, learn, and be happy and be just. The personality, being a part of something greater, has, of course, something greater a part of it. However, the personality may not understand this and the closest communication with the 'something greater' is what psychologists refer to as the subconscious. However, personalities as they evolve who look to mankind for answers and for whatever reason do not look within will become accustomed to responding to mankind's answers.

Now where those answers are of love, there is an immediate cord of response to the most self-centered, or rather personality-centered, individual. So, there is a push and a pull focused upon the personality, which with some personalities, cause them to look within where they face the battle of love and understanding and where victory lies, and some personalities completely reject this inner self and respond and deal much more on Earth's physical level.

Now the personality—all personalities—are destined and are a part of God, no matter what. The personality who is not looking within no matter how difficult the struggle, lives by fear a great deal of time. The personality who just focuses within lives a contemplated self-analytical, and sometimes painful lonely, life.

The Earth experience for the human was meant to be lived joyously. But as in many civilizations, it sometimes is very confusing to see violence, greed, vanity, oppression, and the like around oneself. And with a human experience largely built on fears, there tends to be reinforcement of many fears.

Questions that arise, having lived God's laws, are questions to some of "why me." It indeed takes a wise understanding soul to live God's laws in a world of vanity, violence, greed, lust, fear. But each personality focused on Earth now or in any given experience makes the choice, understanding what they are going to experience. The choice is not made for them but by them.

Now how does one treat a murderer, a violator? There are always going to be laws governing the living in the personality world of the human. And to tell those on Earth what to do would violate one of God's supreme laws, and that would be interfering with free will choice.

There are ways though to justly resolve conflicts on Earth at temporary thought experience. And the supreme method is through seeking to understand God's laws, living God's laws in one's everyday life. That is what the soul wishes for the personality to do. But since this is not always accomplished, man will devise laws, some good, some not so good.

When a soul understands, and before a personality begins to understand great answers follow, wisdom prevails. By choice and attitude, personality and soul achieve destiny. So, accepting your unique power as a human personality to change your world, accepting that individual responsibility will show itself to be wise for your world, and wise for your soul, to interpret for mankind what their laws should be is to inhibit the growth of the experience, the species, the individual fragment personalities. Justice through love will prevail.

Love binds all life on Earth as a part of God, binds all personalities for they are all seeking the same love.

Those who adamantly say they have found it and completely understand it, are not understanding, those who live it, are understanding.

Are there any questions?

Kathleen: No, I have none.

Then love to you.

This is a Wise, Wise, Wise, Wise, Wise One. Imagine you are a visitor from another planet and came upon Earth. Imagine that you understood love's beauty and importance. How would you view the human element?

This is your Wise Guide. That will conclude for tonight. Are there any questions?

Kathleen: No

Then good evening.

✿ LEARNING AND PURPOSE

Wednesday, February 3, 1982, Session 107

This is Jesus.

When I was a child, a voice came to me and told me that I had a mission. My father and mother knew that my coming was for a purpose. My mother, Mary, who they speak of as the Virgin Mary was trained and brought up as an Essene. I, too, was trained as an Essene. I spent much of my growing up on learning with various Essene teachers that spread, or rather stretch, throughout the land. I traveled to many lands to learn the wisdoms from the wise men and wise women.

Understand that I was a man like you and had my purpose unfold before me. I was a man in every respect. I had your doubts, fears, hopes, expectations, and love. I developed no religions. I meant to develop no religions. I spoke for all—all of mankind.

You are speaking and writing of the new age, for the words from your book will be read and interpreted for eons of time.

Mankind will be in its finest hour, for nowhere in your recorded history will there be a more highly evolved people, a more understanding of the laws of God, and the peace and the love that exist within each element of God.

I bless you and will leave you not to return again. I am always with you. Of course, you know that is true.

I AM THAT I AM.

WRITE: This is Jesus. Know thyself and you will know all souls.

Date Unknown

This is Jesus.

I was a man as you and many are men. I was not born in Jerusalem. I was born in Bethlehem and raised in many different locations. I was on the Earth as an old soul and was learning and giving to mankind. My purpose was told to me when I was eighteen. The times were different then and my coming was to bring forth the idea of love on Earth and to fulfill certain scriptures that are part of the Bible. Now there are more Messiahs than the Bible knows, and they come too to bring love and understanding. The time that I came was really a prelude to the time of now, for this begins a new endeavor for mankind not known since the beginning of Earths time, not the same, but a new start, so to speak. Bringing to Earth in verse and words the meaning of Earth's experience and how it is a part of God and God's word. It is a new beginning for mankind since the beginning of Earth's living experience for the human.

A beginning, for it will speak of thought and the supreme thought of love.

You and your family have a Merry Christmas.

Author's Note: The following are other entries; I do not have the recorded dates nor the order in which they were spoken.

🏵 GREATER CONSCIOUSNESS

Notebook #24, Page 3

This is Jesus.

The consciousness is that which is all. When one becomes acquainted with various personalities and becomes fully integrated with all personalities recognizing the validity to the other personalities and the truth that they are no more or less than the soul and are the sum total of the soul's validity, that the need to reincarnate on Earth is no longer. Now soul will still experience something in other existences contributing toward the path of truth.

✿ SIGNIFICANCE OF LIGHT

Notebook # 24, Page 1
This is Jesus. We will now speak of light.

Light, of course, is color, however, all color is not observable. The pure light of energy or energy of light is truth and that is not observable until one seeks within the greater self for truth, love, patience, and understanding, for the sake of the above.

Light of truth or light of being in the natural or conscious-ness state creates what is perceptual and what is perceived from within. Light that is perceived from within is like a feeling of an internal flame that guides one with purpose and direction *(soul consciousness in concert and as an instrument of Divine Guiding Presence).*

Life as humans know it can only exist in creative light of thought.

Through principles of energy, life is manifested through force fields that make up life-giving fields in the physical sense.

Light can cause some problems with those life forms that are not in tune with creative light/life energy.

This life/light energy of which I am speaking, this order of which we speak, relates to solar systems such as the one Earth is a part of.

There are other systems of experience that are in pure light and energy with an understanding of love and that is the order.

Light is the creator of all in truth and love and the giver of all and thereby the receiver of all.

Light energy of truth understands there are variations of light and thought, thought and light, but cannot receive energy that is not of truth. Truth automatically rejects the "light" of untruth.

In light and color in truth, for receipt of an untrue thought through intent is rejected "hands down" so-to-speak, just as oil and water do not mix by nature, so too untruth and truth do not mix, a three-dimensional example only.

HEALING AND MIRACLES

Date Unknown

This is Jesus.

I will now speak of the healing and the miracles that I was credited with performing. I did indeed raise Lazarus from the dead. I did indeed make the blind see. I did indeed make the lame walk. All these things I did in God's name. These were done through thought and thought on the other person's behalf that was keeping them from walking and seeing. The raising of the dead you can do even now with the right person at the right time, for we over here along with the person who is dead will help. All those things you will do in the future. But for now, and the years ahead, you will have just your wisdom, love, understanding and thought. It is not the time for those type of things to occur. You will now just relax and feel your and my God.

PHILOSOPHY, PERCEPTION, AND ENDEAVOR

*The quality of the thought
will determine the vibrational frequency.*

*The soul is focused within a vibrational level itself
and has many component parts or evolving parts of itself,
each part is separate and yet connected to the soul
through thought, love, and will, just as each soul
is connected to greater elements in God by the same.*

CHAPTER 8

PHILOSOPHY, PERCEPTION, AND ENDEAVOR

How do our dreams relate to our reality? Is a thought fleeting or does it exist forever? At what state is the soul connected with the greater self and how does this relate to others? What is the reality of *truth*, when each has their own individual perception?

Within these sessions, souls speak of truth, cycles, and how perception must be measured within the developed structures through order to live *and record* the validity of our experience—that there is an order to everything within this experience—and all experience is part of the evolutionary process of the soul.

The souls speak of what *wanting* is and how Man has redefined it. They speak of where a *want* should come from in order to be of benefit to our experience on Earth.

Souls come forth to speak on the multifaceted nature of *philosophy* and how it symbolizes the vehicle to reach an understanding of our experience.

So, come sit with us.
These messages are meant for you.

(DICTATION BEGINS)

✿ WAKE STATE, DREAM STATE, AND PERCEIVED REALITY

Notebook #33, Page 1
This is a Wise One.

When the soul is in personality, it retains its soul selfness and memory (knowledge). The personality during waking hours is acting out thoughts and they become reality. The sleep state is the method by which the soul makes contact with the Greater Self with the exception of through love. The dream state is one when the soul will be contacted and contact its Greater Self, other internal personalities, friends, and relatives, both on Earth and not on Earth, other personalities and random thoughts. The personality will assimilate this information and symbolize it, which leads to the reality of dreams. The dream state itself is more, or close to true reality, than the waking state of human endeavors.

It is closer to reality because it is less limited by physical restrictions that the earthly body and life places upon it. It is closer because it comes in contact with its Greater Self and the shared reality of truth. Now recognizing that and translating that into an understanding with the context of the physical existence on Earth would take a concerted individual and mass effort. As dreams would be interpreted there would be free will and free thought, and free will interpretation of dreams that would present a multidimensional picture, but would have some mass and shared realities that would bring to light the common beingness of all. Those same truths are on your Earth today presented in a fashion or lived and interpreted in a manner that seems contradictory.

The reasons for this seemingly contradictory nature, within any perceived reality incidentally is the perceiver is viewing the effects of a given experience rather than the intent and meaning. For instance, when one views a creation such as a painting or a building, is the reality the painting, the building, the artist, the architect, the use of the painting or building, the resultant behavior that takes place around and in the work of creativity, the eventual dissolving of the artwork, painting, or building? The perceivers and viewers only see those various effects and each from a different perceptive. The intent and message that is behind the creative endeavor is not seen and known and even that intent has multidimensional aspects to it.

The reality, and only realities, to all expression of God's elements and God, is conveyed and lived and is love, thought, and free will, each existing together as the truth. The shared reality of all has within its beingness these truths. Even the artwork and the building itself express this truth in ways that cannot be visually understood. The beauty and joy of creativity are understood not by beings here upon Earth but by a creator, that in and through truth creates all. The tiniest minutest all or minicell has a part in God's infinite world of love and has an order and validity that is as much a part of all that is as the personality is. This does not mean a building, or an art piece, is the same as a human, nor is a human the same as an animal or an animal the same as a plant in manners of expression, but each is valid and real and a part of all that is or God.

✺ ORDERS AND MEASURING PERCEPTION *(Same Session)*

It is though necessary to measure perception within frameworks and developed structures through order to live and record the validity of experience. All experience is part of the evolutionary process of the soul. The ingredients of this evolutionary process are love, thought, free will, justice, order, and experience as the process itself. Within the human species, there exists the order of the personality and the orders of the human body that make up framework and experience. The personality is that order which reads these words and is a part of the human body through an electrical-magnetical process whereby the colored personality is in with the human body expressing a portion of the evolutionary process of soulness. The order by which all are linked is love.

The soul, that is within the order of plants, is giving love and living out experience by providing food, medicine, and beauty.

The animal order can provide pleasure and beauty in the form of working with mankind through the Earth experience. The animal is not for eating any more than man is.

✿ TRUTH, CYCLES, AND ORDER

Friday, October 15, 1982, Session 246
This is a Wise One.

Each soul upon entering a physical system then evolves through each order and comes to understand through an ordered development that it is part of something greater and more loving with more knowledge and understanding.

A system then is made up of various physical phenomenon cycling and creating and being in an ordered fashion. God is truth and is at the beingness of each element and is the bridge that connects all elements and is the equalness that God created all in and through.

God has been referred to as All one being, a supreme being. However, the supreme being is love, will, and thought. We and you and each are a creation out of truth. Truth bridges all systems and gaps. Truth is. God is. Thought, love, and will are the greatest truth that each possesses and creates through.

When a soul is focusing within a system such as Earth's universe, each soul through truth focuses within all orders at once. Now all orders are a part of and a subject matter to vibrational, physical systems. Each physical element within all systems are because of and through thought. All elements of God are focused then, simultaneously through thought, through will, and through love. All orders of a given system. This occurs in what can be described as mind-time, thought-time, or dream-time, for in it there is only perceived time or through thought, all is occurring now. Thought in varying degrees rules and creates then all physical matter, all vibrational frequencies, within Earth's system or any system. Physical matter and all physical beings or beingness are a reflection of thought created and sustained by and through thought.

Each element then is a reflection of thought, each being is a reflection of thought. Each element, the tiniest infinitesimal element to the largest planet or star, perceives itself as a total being focused in a set of defined order. Each element comes to understand that it passes and is no more than a reflection of a thought.

The physical matter is no longer when the cycle is completed. All physical matter cycles. It was so created through God's mind, and will, and love. All physical matter cycles.

The cycle is predetermined through thought and is set to recycle through thought. All souls are not physical matter. All souls are thought.

Matter dissolves, for it is a reflection and is born again unto matter through a physical cycle based upon thought, love, and will. The dream which is matter will pass away to minds that evolve to understand their true nature, then the mind is set free from the laws of matter. The matter will continue to function and cycle as long as there is the desire to have the matter. Master souls coordinate and work with systems to develop cycles and to develop experience for evolving souls. Master souls are made up of many, many minds that are in concert and singular will through perceived truth and understanding and that are as free as they have evolved to understand. Master souls have been on as mass Gods, as beings of guidance and truth, and as warring beings fighting truth. All to the evolving being is a matter of perception and need and justice.

We will continue tomorrow evening.

PERCEPTION, THOUGHT, AND REALITY

Sunday, October 17, 1982, Session 248
This is a Wise One.

When the soul then is focused within any reality it is focused by the method of thought creation, the infinite law of God, and truth says that which is created through thought lives forever as a free will creation. These creations become charged with sound and color at various frequencies. They remain forever. Thoughts then are realities that exist, that know not what they are or where they go unless they are created so.

To believe or accept that each of your thoughts and the soul's thoughts live forever is not required or necessary. But we assure you that all thoughts live forever. The cosmos is made up and created entirely of thought. That is the reality. The perception is by individual creations and their observation of all about them.

Thoughts carry sound, vibration, frequency, and are marked by color. Each thought carries its own energy and seeks to accumulate more energy lest it becomes alive but at a very, very low vibration rate.

Thoughts have infinite life, but thoughts are not free will spirits in the sense that the soul is. Thoughts live forever and are created and reacted by thoughts on a similar vibrational plain. But all thoughts touch all beings, for perception and intent are quite different in many cases. Each thought perceives itself as the total creation and lives forever perceiving that, eventually slowing its vibration rate to a very low vibration rate, but never the less, it remains forever. Some thoughts remain at high vibration rates forever picked up again and again by other energy sources or elements of God and used. This relates to laws of physics, however, physics that cannot be measured by human physicists. It is beyond the sight of the human, beyond the perception of the human.

Each element of God then functions based upon perception. Each element created in and for an evolving cycle remains evolving forever. The soul which brings about elements is tied to evolving cycles until it becomes at one with God and steps aside from the evolutionary process and becomes a pure, pure, creator. Therefore, each element of God while evolving to greater and lesser degrees defends its validity and beingness and by not letting go, it ties the soul to it. The soul, the greater mind of each, will eventually reason and think and break the ties. But in so doing it takes with it valid memories of what it has learned that are stored forever and goes on to become a co-creator.

Souls then create through thought and are thought. Thought is not emotion or senses or color or vibration, thought creates. Thought is the soul. Thought gives always when it has learned and evolved for it recognizes that one cannot hold onto what one can never possess and yet by giving it, one has it forever. Reality then is a belief in what you are. The You can be reading this now or be an idle thought. What each is, is a creation by thought that is thought at different vibrational levels that will live forever. Thought is being. Souls create beings.

Perception and reality then are always interrelated for the perception is the reality to the perceiver and the reality is the perception of the functioning element. As any system is, there are many elements that go to make it up. Each element relates to the system through perception. Each system is a perception of greater elements. Perceptions pass away in truth for there is just truth.

In summary, all that has been created is perceiving individually until truth is understood.

That will conclude for this evening.

❀ ENDEAVOR

Monday, October 18, 1982, Session 249
This is a Wise One.

The endeavor is the experience. Love for the endeavor and you will find many rewards and great satisfaction. Love for the reward and you will be left wanting.

Each element comes about through a thought process. The thought process can be intended or reactive. The endeavor is doing. The endeavor is living. The endeavor is what evolving is about. For only through endeavor does one come to learn and understand. The endeavor is related to perception and reality, also. The endeavor is the action of perception and reality in an evolving system. Thought brings about the endeavor. When the endeavor is purposeful, it is creative. When the endeavor is a reaction, it is frustration. When one pursues an endeavor with purpose, the frustrations will be there but will be dealt with and handled so that the purpose can be achieved. When one is reacting and doing out of reaction, then one is being led from endeavor to endeavor, struggle to struggle.

Purpose is manifested within. Purpose is learned and understood from within. When one relates more to what others think and create, one pursues reactive endeavors. When one relates inwardly to any endeavor and ties it to personal purpose, one will achieve inner peace and rewards through time.

Endeavor and purpose as we have said are related to perception and reality in an evolving system. The purpose and endeavor will be perceived and acted upon differently by uniquely evolving beings.

Each system has many systems within it. Each universe has many worlds within it. Each system has many orders. Each order has many elements of God. Perception of what the endeavor is and purpose is aligned with Christ thinking. Through the alignment of endeavor and purpose, one *becomes* through reality, more in *one* through endeavor.

Endeavors can be assigned rules that change in time, change in perception. The greatest rule that one will come to understand is to love for the endeavor. There are some very basic and logical and truthful reasons for loving for the endeavor. They relate to happiness and peace and love.

That will conclude for this evening.

Tuesday, October 19, 1982, Session 250
This is a Wise One.

The simplicity of endeavor is that there, in greater and lesser degrees, is always an endeavor. Man has pursued various endeavors that have created mankind's structures, philosophies, and rules. The endeavor, the intent, the thought behind all, measure justly so, growth for the soul structures, philosophies, rules, all change from one society to another. There will always be the living of life, the endeavor, and that too relates directly to perceptive or perception. It is the living of the endeavor, not the endeavor that marks *just* evolution. The endeavor is merely set in time, which in terms of soul, does not exist. The quality of thought in action and even reaction is what is measured when one is evaluating evolutionary understanding. Through the endeavor, one is presented with an opportunity to live according to God's laws and to express through endeavor.

The endeavor then is especially important to all evolving elements for it expresses creativity, expresses love, expresses understanding, expresses development, expresses the progress of the soul. The endeavor is action. Behind the endeavor is thought. Thought projects and becomes involved in the endeavor. Each element contributes to making up greater endeavors that are within various levels of understanding. Becoming involved in an endeavor is all what we have said and yet the endeavor itself, we remind you, is but a reflection of a thought. The thought behind the endeavor relates directly to creation. So, each and all are creating in greater and lesser degrees. Each views the process and results from an individual perspective.

The endeavor itself is many times interpreted as truth, but endeavors change. Truth is to come within perception and endeavor to enlightenment, and truth is to have awareness and understanding and to touch the element of God that is behind all. It is through endeavor that understanding is found, personal endeavor, the living and experiencing and learning and understanding, of what is true happiness and peace. Behind all endeavor and understanding lies the truth of love, thought, and will.

That will conclude this section.

✿ PHILOSOPHY: THE VEHICLE TO UNDERSTANDING

Tuesday, October 19, 1982, Session 250, Page 2
We will now write of philosophy, the vehicle to understanding.

Philosophy is the vehicle by which thought expresses before the action-element of endeavor. Philosophy, too, is tied to perception and creativity and truth. Philosophy is interpretation. Philosophy can generally be said to be understanding. Philosophy, too, is a reflection of thought. Philosophy is a perception of all elements that go to make up beings and beingness. Philosophy is a broad-based term that brings about idea construction and it becomes endeavors, perceptions, and becomes the thinking understanding process that works with and through endeavor.

Philosophy belongs to all elements of God. Each element has degrees of understanding of their current philosophy. Using the human personality, it can arrive at a philosophy based upon its focus and perception within and about endeavor and life. Philosophy can be expanded upon when the human personality touches the element that exists within, that is their higher awareness, self, and soul. Within each human personality is the soul that has created it. And within each soul is God. Philosophy develops and alters at points of perception then. But again, philosophy is a reflection of thought. When one is thinking they are expressing and developing philosophies that become endeavors.

That is all for this evening.

Wednesday, October 20, 1982, Session 251

Philosophy can be multifaceted or biopic in nature. Each human has a philosophy inherent within them. For in the evolutionary development of the soul or mind the occurrences of understanding are focused in the mind not necessarily just upon Earth. However, the soul is on a path of learning truth focused within any reality. So, philosophies may assume or maintain perspectives and become the guideposts for living, existing, and evolving. Endeavor is the actual experiencing. Philosophy is the method or transportation for the thought. Thought is the creative element. All interrelate. All focus and are perceptive in perception.

Philosophy is of the mind and is the method in transport for developing governments, religions, earthly structures. All is unique individual perspectives, each having free will yet focused and defined by the experience. Each has free will but being tied to philosophy, religion, endeavor, being tied to that prevents the exercise of free will. The intent and purpose for experience within any reality is to find a home with God. God is found through truth, love given, thought, and free will.

The soul then is thought. It assimilates thought and acquires experience and comes to understand and perceive based upon experience and assimilation of thoughts. The mind projects to create and to experience. The mind is always thinking. Thought is given and thought is received. The mind assimilates and/or projects and holds those thoughts that are valuable until there comes a greater understanding and realization that nothing has to be held. The mind is ever growing and ever shrinking and ever expanding at once, creating its own truths until infinite truth and God are understood. At that time the mind need not project for there is nothing more to defend. The mind need not hold when there is nothing more to hold.

Now, there is still some projection, for lack of a better word, or some emission of thought. It is given in truth and pure love. It needs not be defended, it needs not be defined, it is, just truth. The creation of that mind is in pure given and pure love.

Understanding that it is justly receiving it will receive all that is valid and have all that is necessary or required to sustain it.

Its greatest reward is to give. It receives only when it gives. Its purpose is to be truth. It has nothing to prove for it is in truth. It accepts what it cannot change and changes what it cannot accept when focused within an experience. It is individual and all at once. It is evolved to a state of love and truth. And only good for that is what it emits surrounds it. It is at once understanding, patient, compassionate, and loving. Truth realizes and understands that; that which is given is received and gives only what it wishes to receive through understanding.

IN TRUTH AND GOD (Same Session)

Now all evolving minds must and will interpret until awareness and understanding unfold, each project, accepts and responds to another based upon need. Truth has no unfulfilled needs and yet receives all goodness, for truth projects all goodness. Truth works in all phases and gives in love what each wish to receive, accepts from another only that which it needs, and needs nothing; for in truth it is already part of all and another.

To describe and define what is the mind is done by each through perception. To describe and define how diverse and multidimensional the mind is, is to describe by perception. The mind belongs to each and all. In truth the mind is all, and each that has arrived at truth recognizes the allness that exists. Truth is within each element of God. And the mind projects and defends and perceives and creates and undoes and unfolds until it reaches truth. The mind of God then creates each and is within each, and each has been created in God's likeness equally, each endowed with God's love.

Then God desired companionship and created equally all and each to be with God, creating with God, forever loving. Each creation knew the principles, knew what they were, and yet only through giving could they come to understand that they were within all and yet themselves. Each will be with God in truth and that decision is made when it is realized that it is not meant to be alone.

The soul or fragment-mind will admit being a mind with and in God. The final, or the understanding steps to God are through

225

the law, and the law is the will of God, and the will of God is love, and the justice given in love is that each and all can and will receive what is given. Thus, sayeth the Lord.

Truth knows no time, truth is infinite as God is infinite, as God is truth, as love is—and is in all—and infinity knows no time, it just is. And an experience, an endeavor in perception in creating the time recognized or not, is always now the choice, is always that is the sum total in the mind of all pasts and all futures and yet in love he shall receive and that he has sown and reap the benefits justly so before understanding transcends, becomes, and evolves to in, and for, and to be truth.

DEATH AND REINCARNATION

*When one leaves the Earthly body,
one is allowed to see what one needs.*

*In your Earthly body, each has a
responsibility to each and that
responsibility is love, understanding,
compassion, resolve, purpose.*

CHAPTER 9

DEATH AND REINCARNATION

What happens when one leaves the body? What is it like "over there"? Is there something beyond this Earth experience? Do we all reincarnate? Do we reincarnate with the same friends and relatives as in this life? In the following sessions, souls and loved ones speak of the death experience, answering commonly asked questions and provide a simple, yet profound look into life on Earth and beyond.

So, come sit with us.
These messages are meant for you.

(DICTATION BEGINS)

❀ WHEN ONE LEAVES THE EARTHY BODY

Friday, October 16, 1981, Session 22
This is a Wise One.

When one leaves the Earthly body, one is allowed to see what one needs. If that be a Jesus, a relative, a St. Peter at a gate, they will be presented that image. Relatives often congregate to meet a soul. For in many experiences they have a pact going back to many incarnations to review what they have accomplished for their purpose or purposes.

Relatives and friends do contact some Earthly people. This is done for purposes of enlightenment that you will not fear death and that this is eternal life and love.

We go through learning experiences and environments here. They are of our own choosing and understanding. The essence here has a greater understanding of its purpose and where it is in its evolutionary pattern. It varies from essence to essence. Some have trouble leaving Earthly experiences because their structures are not evolved to make the transition easier. Reality here is beautiful and relief for Earthly bondage. Those essences or souls who do not understand this, evolve more slowly.

❀ SOUL AND HUMAN EXPERIENCE *(Same Session)*

This is Mike Rice.

I am learning much. *(Mike Rice was one of the souls who spoke when the sessions first began.)* Do you have any questions about life here? I am learning about *true* life, which the human experience is a part of that. It is limited only to the degree that I allow it to be limited. Perception and knowledge are a part of the evolutionary being to the degree that I understand it is enlightening. I was speaking for my essence and myself. All is a part of my essence and all is a part of all.

I will help. We evolve into a positive purpose and enlightenment and where this is not possible you evolve how you evolve, and I will evolve how I will evolve. If you remember this, humans, in your dealings with other humans and other animals you may find harmony. You will also find a more accelerated evolvement of your soul or essence. This is difficult in the human experience in the evolutionary process of mankind. Man is wrought within with structures defining where man can want to go. One cannot say "you do what I do, for I am right."

We are all in this evolutionary process together. Some of us more enlightened than others. It is always a responsibility of each essence, whether here or on Earth, to learn and understand the nature of the evolutionary experience and how all are a part of God or all that is. In your Earthly body, each has a responsibility to each, and that responsibility is love, understanding, compassion, resolve, purpose. Each has a responsibility to their evolutionary process, also. Each has to realize that each is a part of all. That each is also self-evolving.

❀ THE MIND (Same Session)

This is a Wise One.

The mind was created by God and through evolution created by the individual essence. The mind remembers knowledge and some soul experiences when the mind is in harmony with the soul or essence. The mind is not always in harmony with the soul or essence. The mind remembers knowledge—structures—soul minds are of a learned nature. Some are of or less rigid or less learned nature. All mind will eventually learn truth. The mind is a tool to use during or after your earthly experience. The mind is only a part of the essence is all and is a part of all that is.

Creation is a work of all, for all are a part of God and God, I Am a part of all. Know this: I Am That I Am—Believe that you and the individual essence, soul, energy—you have within you—power, understanding, and love, to know that I Am That I Am. This soul known as Michael in this life will let all know this essence, energy, soul human potential, and that is love, love, love, for I created all out of love.

(Kathleen's Note: Mike's finger points out and his body stiffens with the head going back and then begins to jerk and relax a little, head jerking side to side.)

This is Seth. The mind is a portion of free will. The mind is a portion of the soul or essence within all humans lies the inner reality of creation, love, God.

Write—This is God, The God of Light, Love, Understanding, Creation.

❀ DEATH EXPERIENCE: EINSTEIN SPEAKS

Session 29
This is Einstein.

Death is a pleasant experience. One is met by whomever one needs to be met by. One will be met by Jesus if that is appropriate or by a devil if that is what is needed. One may be met by both. One may be met by friends, enemies, relatives, or whomever one wishes to be met by at the death experience. One is then allowed to rest for a period of time to truly realize that they are no longer trapped in a physical body. The learning and experiencing here begin. There is no stress, and one only chooses to reincarnate after understanding what they wish to accomplish in physical form.

The period of time varies from soul to soul. There are exceptions. One is allowed to select parents and this is usually agreed upon by the parent before either has reincarnated. Now there is the advantage of free will and the mind, which sometimes causes things to change.

Soulmates may not meet at the right time or not at all. This changes the play or acts on Earth somewhat, but as has been said I am sure this is an infinite evolution and eventually plays or debts are acted out by the human bodies. Again, I stress, it is up to the souls; you are not controlled by anyone else. You make your own choice. It is all up to you. This is why attitude in physical life is so important. A positive attitude helps you direct your life in concert with your soul or essence objective.

That is all.

❀ LIFE OVER THERE

Monday, November 9, 1981, Session 42
This is Mike Rice.

Hello good friends. Do you have any questions before I begin to talk of life over there?

Mike: No, speak of life over there.

When one first arrives here any number of things can occur. One can be greeted by relatives, by enemies, by a Jesus, or a Devil, or a St. Peter.

One will be allowed to adjust, and the greeting is based upon one's belief when they arrive.

There at one time or another is a union that takes place between old souls that the one leaving has known. At that time, depending upon the awareness of the soul, a number of things will be explained, and some instruction will begin and some help regarding directing this newly arrived soul. The soul at first is guided, and realities are created for the soul to make them comfortable.

The soul is taught to realize that they have creative powers and can create their own reality.

They will create a reality they are comfortable in, it may change over what you call time depending upon the soul's needs.

There are psychodramas that are created here for the further development of the soul. In a reincarnational sense that is what the Earth incarnation is, a psychodrama.

There is happiness and love for those souls who seek it and understanding that life is love. There is sadness and pain and confusion for those who are still locked in a three-dimensional philosophy.

A reincarnation is chosen for the essence, by the essence, with guidance from wise ones. The essence when arriving will assume usually their last earthly incarnation. The essence may assume, or eventually will assume, a picture they have of their self, based upon total reincarnational personalities.

There are different levels of development for the soul or essence. These have, or there are I understand, about seven levels. Each level has a wiser and greater understanding of purpose.

When one chooses to reincarnate they, in most cases, make that choice with other souls that they wish to enter, react with, or pay a debt with, too.

There are a group of souls who enter bodies to achieve a purpose.

Parents are chosen, sometimes the parents have reincarnated early to carry out an agreed reincarnational situation, like a mother and father or a mother and child changing rolls from one reincarnational role to another.

A soul automatically advances or grows to a greater step of reality when they have acquired a larger base of understanding.

Life here is not unlike certain situations on Earth other than there is not the stress here, for the most part. There is a greater understanding that love is truth and that life is infinite.

When souls reenter earth situations they adopt a mind to develop a new personality. They also have soul memories relating to past personalities.

Some will deny and fight those memories and refer to them as inner conflicts.

They will try and adapt to other three-dimensional concepts having their existence dictated by others. Some will look within and come to a realization that they hold the key to power and success on Earth.

PURPOSE FOR RE-ENTERING EARTH LIFE *(Same Session)*

There is always a purpose for re-entering an earth life. This purpose is usually not a singular purpose, but rather a group of purposes consisting of soul purpose, debt purpose, and love or contribution to all that is purpose.

Most enter for debt purpose. More enlightened and experienced souls recognize debt, but have personal purpose, and wise souls such as you enter for the purpose of God.

End of dictation. Are there any questions?

Mike: No questions.

I bid you a fond good evening and give you my love.

AFTERLIFE TRANSITION

Friday, November 27, 1981, 10 P.M., Session 59

This is a Wise One. We will speak of the afterlife transition and what it entails.

Recall that acceleration, velocity, frequency and color marks that soul and the energy that forms all life. When leaving the human body there is a gradual raising of vibration and frequency like being lifted into the air. The greater the frequency, the quicker the motion and time no longer exist as you know it. This has been understood by some other civilizations that would far pre-date your civilization your three-dimensional terms. Once upon leaving, the human body becomes initially what they perceive and visualize themselves to be.

Some chose a younger look initially remembering their best physical state. Others may be older, and visualize themselves that way. Some in your terms, stay near Earth for a while understanding that they are still alive but looking and seeing that the body they had known was lifeless.

✿ IN SUDDEN DEATH *(Same Session)*

In a situation where one dies suddenly like an accident, they sometimes do not fathom that they have in fact in physical Earth terms "died" and many in fact remain near Earth not immediately understanding what to do. When one leaves the physical body, there is a great frequency change and they then might meet a relative still here, a friend still here and even an enemy from physical association.

It greatly depends on the understanding of the personality and ego portion at the time of their so-called "death." Souls whether here, or on Earth, or in another alternative experience are not always aware entirely of their Greater Self and their truly infinite being, and their relationship to their God. This is learned through many experiences. Whether here or in another alternative experience the process is learning, understanding, battling, for that infinite wisdom that manifests the soul's true nature, and in all souls that nature, that thought, is Love.

✿ BEYOND EARTH EXPERIENCES *(Same Session)*

This is a Wise One.

You should know that there is more than the Earth experience. There are other experiences and that Earthly incarnations are repeated until the soul reaches the understanding of its true being. And the Earth experience, the human experience is no longer necessary. A whole new set of experiences is pursued by the soul to continue to grow. In learning, in all experience, over here, where there may be more rest and contemplation the key in determining destiny is through attitude whether a learned and correct attitude or a misunderstood and incorrect attitude exist. Where negativity and egocentricity are prevalent, there is a greater battle, for there are more structures, fears, guilts to overcome. Souls tend to attract like-souls. Souls are colored differently when there is great negativism, depression, and misunderstanding. But all souls are a part of God. ALL, ALL is a part of God.

And at the core of being in all souls, there is that infinitely infallible understanding, patient resolve that exists in all, from the most knowledgeable and wisest to the most unknowledgeable. For God forsakes no soul. The so call "Hells" you refer to are made from within.

Author's Note: Within a number of sessions, two loved ones who had passed requested and were allowed to speak through my father. They came forth to share their love, what it is like 'over there,' and to reassure our family that they were okay. I share this personal experience because I feel that their words are beautiful, and their messages can bring comfort.

Friday, November 27, 10 P.M., Session 59
Loved One: Bert, Author's Fraternal Grandmother's Husband
This is Bert. I wish to say that there is only life and to say that love is greater than I knew, and I have spoken to Julia *(Author's fraternal great-grandmother)* and she is happy and busy and a wise soul here.

(Bert speaking to Author's grandmother) We have been together before on Earth, and if we chose, will be together again on Earth. I do know that when we are ready, and it is advisable and beneficial; we will again reincarnate.

The experiences here are similar to Earth's without stress; it depends on the soul. There is much learning and many things to see, but one can relax if one enjoys something as simple as golf, it can be done. In this state, I can be what I wish, but there is so much love and understanding that I'm compelled to learn. But I have been told it is up to me. Others help me; there are guides and teachers here to help. The atmosphere one wishes can be had by thinking it. It is not quite that simple, but there are those who help me to understand that. I must go now. Love to you.

Monday, September 21, 1981, Evening
Kathleen: It was on this evening, through Mike that the Guides said that my Dad, Art, would contact me on Sunday, September 27, at 1:00 in the afternoon while our kids played in the rec room. He wanted to let me know that he was okay. The Guides also told me that it was my Dad who came to see me one night as I was going to sleep. I was staying at my Mom's house that particular night when, just as I was going to sleep, a man's face that I did not recognize came above me; it was hazy, and he looked directly at me close to my face. It startled me, and I screamed really loud. The Guide said that my Dad was trying to contact me to talk, but he wasn't ready—it was too soon, which could explain the haziness and why I did not recognize him.

Sunday, September 27, 1981, 1 P.M.
Loved One: Art, Author's Maternal Grandfather
This is Art. How are you? I am fine. I love you.

Tell Bill *(Kathleen's brother; Author's Uncle)* there is no death. There is only love. That I am fine and there is only eternal life.

Kathleen to her Dad: Dad, what happened at the moment of your death?

Art: It was painless. There's no death Kathy, it was painless. I just saw a white light and then it was like still being there, and knowing you were not there. I could see Mike and Mary (Art's wife). I could see Kathy and Bill. I could see all—all that took place. I could see and watch. Things are peaceful here. One goes through a re-entry phase in order to become accustomed to one's true nature—Soul nature.

One has a learning process here and it is wise. It is very wise. One has a wonderful feeling of love here—indescribable.

I will not be visiting you many more times. I will be preparing to re-enter human form.

Wednesday, September 30, 1981, 10 P.M.
Loved One: Art, Author's Maternal Grandfather
This is Art. I will be reincarnated in November of 1982. I am looking forward to my earthly reincarnation. I love you all. All. I love you. I must go now good evening.

Saturday, October 3, 1981, 10 P.M.
Loved One: Art, Author's Maternal Grandfather
This is Art. How are you? I am fine. This will be the last time that I speak with you. I must prepare for the big event. Until the big event, love to you. Dad
   (My mother started to cry.)
   Art: Please do not cry.
   Kathleen: I am fine.
   Art: Good.
   Love Happiness.
   This is your Wise Guide. To your wife, your father is now with other wise ones preparing for his quote-unquote "big event."
   Author's Note: Later my mother talked to the Guides and she said that it was her understanding that before one reincarnates they can choose time, place, and cause of death and if so, did her father choose? (Art died at age 55 of cancer.)
   Wise One's Response: I am familiar with the personality known as Art. And he indeed did decide to die when even choosing the matter of his death. If he were living in a past time when plagues were a convenient way to die, and he was, he might have chosen to die that way.

✿ WAITING FOR THE DEATH OF THE BODY

Monday, December 14, 1981, Session 72
This is a Wise One.
   We will speak of waiting for the death of the body.
   When one feels that they are going to die or leave this physical existence in the near future and they have accepted that, there usually is a gradual withdrawing of the energy force known as the soul. The personality will remain until it accepts leaving the physical body. The personality stays with the body and is still

connected to the greater soul until the death of the body occurs or there is no longer any use to remain in the body.

At the moment of a prepared death, a personality gains wisdom that it has not known before and in fact does see its life flash before it and then not realizing that they have died, remain near the body, or realizing that they have died and feeling so relieved, rapidly depart. Or they are a knowledgeable soul who immediately goes to its integrated level to resume learning.

Now there is absolutely no pain the moment of death or just before death for then the focus is on the Greater Self and the transition. Some remain near their body not knowing what to do or where to go. In such cases, a wise one usually comes forth and aids the soul in finding the Greater Self. When the soul understands that it can no longer function in the now dead body, it will begin the process of learning.

Now there may have to be other transitional stages like a Heaven or Hell or purgatory, or other descriptive term created by the departing soul. When learning begins at the lower levels, there is not a great deal of difference between physical existence and this new learning experience.

WHEN PERSONALITY DEPARTS THE BODY

Thursday, December 17, 1981, Session 75
This is a Wise One.

The nature of the soul is such that when the soul is born out of love and forged with free will, it is born with basic instincts of love and creating.

The creating out of love is the goal and when a soul manifests a personality in the Earth's sphere, the personality is forged with free will. Now, this may be more than one personality at a time. Now there is always a greater consciousness outside of Earth sphere. There is the greater individual soul for each fragment belonging to that soul and there is infinite loving consciousness.

Now when personality departs the human body and returns, it is greeted by friends and loved ones and when upon gaining some form of reuniting with the Greater Self, a decision about reincarnation will exist within that soul and that soul may choose to reincarnate and learn, taking with it any lessons from teachings.

The soul then finally accepts all the individual personalities, then truth is achieved and the necessity of incarnating on Earth is achieved. At that time, the soul will have gone through many incarnations on Earth and lived the justice of reincarnation and had begun to reap the fruits of their labor.

THE DECISION TO REINCARNATE

Monday, March 1, 1982, Session 127
This is a Wise One.

When the soul reincarnates it first goes through a rest and learning period if the soul chooses. Now the physical Earthly existence is a true challenge meant for those hardy souls to more quickly accelerate learning. This is also true of other physical type experiences in other systems. Souls often incarnate with like souls that associate over periods, more so civilizations.

Now when the decision to enter is made, there are guides that will guide the personality. Souls usually spend time between Earthly endeavors studying and understanding and learning. When a soul projects upon Earth a portion of itself, it creates a new organism.

————gap————*Kathleen: Mike is dozing off again.*————

When the soul chooses, a series of choices are made by the soul; the choice to enter having been made, the circumstances of birth having been determined, a projection occurs.

EPILOGUE

There is one thing for certain that you can gather from these sessions, whether your life has been fairly smooth or full of bumps, you are among the hardiest of souls who have consciously chosen this life in form. Your willingness to accelerate your learning, despite the stress and emotional rollercoaster this life promises, is an act of pure faith for which not all are ready. Yet here you are. Your search for deeper meaning and purpose is a sign that you innately know of this divine love within you and your connection with God. Through this, you are infinitely guided to finding the answers that you seek and the healing that you need.

As you see meaning within these sessions with Spirit, you begin to discover ways to free yourself of karmic patterns that no longer serve your soul and your life here and now. You begin to break free of obsessive thought and "victim" mentality that this conditioned experience seems to encourage, with the knowing of the supreme truth of love, from which you were created to live and be. You may discover a renewed energy flowing through your life and a clearer path to joy.

I reflect regularly on the three fundamental truths each are forged with upon entering this life for the purpose of learning and creating—love, thought and free will. With these, you are empowered to transform any undesirable aspects of your life in companionship with God, our Divine Guiding Presence, and quite possibly create new, wholly beneficial experiences unforeseen upon your birth. You have the opportunity to heal areas of your life that need the most mending, which in turn heals you as deep as your soul, furthering your evolution into the infinite divine state of dynamic love, mercy, grace, and compassionate wisdom.

Spirit reminds you that you have all of the creative empowerments necessary to create the wholly beneficial life you desire and the constant companionship of other loving souls, and God, to help guide you to healing, purpose, enlightenments, and wholeness. From this day forward, upon utilizing your forged love, thought and free will, you can make wholly beneficial conscious decisions that indeed transform your life for the better.

Wholly beneficial conscious decisions are decisions made from a place where who you are, as "knower" soul, lovingly merges with your life as "personality" here and now on Earth. There will inevitably be moments in life where you are faced with making exponentially difficult decisions that you know will affect not only your life but the life of others and even the path of your soul. And in these times, it is especially important to utilize your free will in the most purely loving, compassionate way and in prayer and companionship with God and all souls involved. In these challenging times, you are brought beyond simply utilizing your free will to choose and create the outcome. You now know that you can step into a higher energy field of love and co-creation by making decisions that are wholly beneficial for you in your life.

I would like to complete with a snippet of one of the sessions with a Wise One from Chapter One. As you read it, I wish for you to read it as if it were your own words. We all share a common thread—the *I am that I am.*

I Am that I Am.
I Am the beginning.
I Am the ending.
I Am never ending.
I Am that I Am.
In the beginning, there is no beginning, but there is I Am.
There is a thought of love.

There is a soul of love.
There are infinite souls that are a part of the I Am,
and each is forged with LOVE,
and each is forged with CREATING,
and each is forged with FREE WILL.
The love that each and all consciousness possess
is the seed of being.
The love that all possess is the seed of creation.
I Am that I Am.
When one understands the nature of love,
then one becomes a part of I Am that I Am.
I Am that I Am has the love for all
at the seed of I Am that I Am.
That which the soul gives is returned,
and that which the soul gives is an expression of love.

I Am. That I am.
   God Bless.

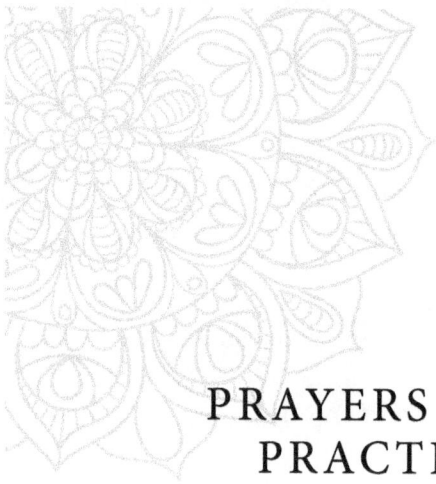

PRAYERS AND LOVE'S PRACTICE HEART MEDITATION

After I read all of the sessions shared in this book, I genuinely wondered how I could implement what I learned into my life, so that I may have a greater connection with God and my higher state of being and gain more clarity and clearer guidance moving forward. In response, I created these meditations and prayers that I now want to share with you. (For more practices, meditations and prayers, visit www.LoveIsTheSeed.com)

In meditation and prayer, we relax into the divine guiding centering field of aware knowing that is beyond thinking or emotions. On the other side of that still guiding silence within our soul, there are various enlightenments. I have included a special heart meditation and two daily prayers that you can implement starting today, to begin taking you into this space of enlightenment.

❀ Heart Meditation: The Heart Holds All Answers

Love's Practice is a Five-Step Heart Meditation designed to be a relaxing practice, simply giving attention to the heart. The heart is both intelligent and loving and works with all systems within the body. When the heart and mind are aligned, Soul as "knower," can utilize both for guidance and healing. The more frequent our practice, the greater our ability to access this intelligence.

Begin by sitting in a comfortable position and close your eyes. For just this moment, let go of your thoughts and the outside world. I like to preface this meditation with a prayer: *"God show me Thy heart in my heart and my heart as a part of Thy heart."*

Focus your attention on your heart and the space surrounding your heart. Focus on feeling the beating of your heart, and relax.

While gently resting your attention on your heart center, take a few deep breaths, then slow your breathing to where it feels comfortable.

Within this rhythm of breath and beat, softly from within ask your heart for any answers or messages to be revealed to you.

For the next five or ten minutes, relax with this intention. As you do so, you will begin to feel newer energy—perhaps healing or loving or understanding/knowing—move through you and your body.

You may also see glimpses of objects or visions. Let the experience be what it is. If you begin "thinking" or drift off to sleep, notice it and then bring your attention back to your heart center.

Upon completing each meditation, reflect on and document any feelings, scents, and visions that you experienced. Keep a log, formal or informal, of each meditation. By doing so, you will begin to see a theme or a pattern emerging, or gradual ease in connection and flow. Then attend to tasks at hand. More and more you will feel a newer, vitalizing healing and loving energy move through you.

❀ *Prayer: You Are Infinitely Guided*

The power of prayer relies on the knowing that our Divine Guiding Presence for which we are a part is always at work for our benefit. This Divine Presence is always present and our greatest companion. When we pray, we acknowledge the divine within ourselves and our connection to All. Prayers are always answered. Unanswered prayers do not exist. Although there are times where we feel that our prayers are not being answered or in times that we may feel alone, we are infinitely guided in "right timing" and always for our benefit.

❀ Love's Daily Prayer

This is a prayer of acceptance of love. To love thyself as perfect, whole and complete. To love thyself as God loves you, for to have faith in yourself, is to have faith in God. To love thyself is to love God. It is a prayer to open yourself to the answers within, ever connected to and answered in companionship with the radiant resonant light of Divine Guiding Presence.

Today,
May my heart be filled with
the profound Love from which I was created.
May I fully accept all answers
to be clearly revealed to me and all needs met.
May I relax in the knowing
that for every step I take today
You are taking ninety-nine steps for my benefit.
May I accept Love, from myself and others,
and be filled with all of the joys this life gifts me.
And may I be of service to others today and empowered by
the radiant light of Love, Grace, Mercy and Compassionate Wisdom
from which I was created to live and be.

By Lisa Hromada
Love is the Seed: Teachings from the Spirit World

Now rest for a moment on the powerful words you just put forth and let the energy they carry, flow in and through you. Then go about your day's tasks and notice any messages, answers, or inner knowing that may arise. And when it does, no matter how small, say "thank you" within yourself, knowing that indeed for every one step you take, God takes ninety-nine steps for your benefit.

 * If you choose to do this prayer at the end of the day, reflect briefly on the day, give thanks, and then set the intention of the night's dreams: *"God, Jesus, Higher Self, I relax in your presence and give thanks for today. May any and all answers of benefit to me now, be revealed to me tonight and may I wake refreshed."*

❀ Gratitude Prayer

One of the greatest privileges is for us as soul to come into human form and experience this life in companionship with other souls and in companionship with the Love from which we were all created. This simple daily prayer of gratitude is intended to take us closer to the vibrational energy that encompasses the clear enlightening presence of love, grace, compassionate wisdom, and the giver of empowerments.

Upon completing the prayer, rest for a moment and listen to any thoughts, feelings or sensations that may arise, and then go about your tasks, knowing that you are, indeed, always in the presence of and a part of Divine love.

Gratitude Prayer

God, thank you for the ways in which you showed your love to me today,
through the kindness and service of others, for the ability
to accomplish all that I did today, and for the gift of my loved ones.
For this I am grateful.
I may not have noticed all of the ways you showed your constant
companionship to me,
but I know you walked alongside of me today and are always with me
forevermore.
For this I am grateful.
Thank you to those, who unbeknownst to me, contribute to
making the world, my world, a better place.
For this I am grateful.
Thank you for this day, for my health, for my safety, and for my
abundance.
Thank you for your guiding presence and your constant companionship,
love, grace, mercy, and healing.
From the depths of my heart, I am grateful.

By Lisa Hromada
Love is the Seed: Teachings from the Spirit World

DEFINITIONS

Color – the marking of souls and thoughts—visually speaking; light reflected

Energy – electro-magnetic and electro-chemical vibrations and manifestations marked by color

Entity – a group of souls, forming a like-mind and purpose. The entity is a group of souls from various levels and orders for a given purpose. Souls bind together for just (justice) reasons for the development of the entity or the soul

Evolution – the gaining of understanding through experience and growth

Fragment – a portion of; reflection; personality "fragment" (portion of the personality); that portion of a soul focused in experience; soul can also be defined as a fragment (portion) of the "whole" that is God, and a fragment of the whole of all souls/consciousness; also a fragment (or portion) of a soul can focus within its reality/experience, that is for the human mind; "Divine mind" is awareness enlightenments

God – Creator; manifest in all that is—the "I Am"

Involution – the gaining of understanding through inward experience and growth

Justice – receiving what one has given; karma, reincarnation, receiving, giving, understanding that—that which the souls give is returned

Love – All; God; grace, mercy, compassionate wisdom, giving; that which frees you; that which is inherent in our being; that which we are created from; foundation for all creation

Order – all manifestations that go to make up the evolutionary experience: man, animals, etc. Order has a great natural law: the part benefits the whole and the whole the part. It is part of a divine flow: unity > harmony > order > balance > symmetry that flow from the original light of God. Everything has a function and all life is ensouled. There are orders within orders—think of what needs to function, in order, within one bodily organ to make it function, which then aids other elements in the body to function—each having their own order of functioning. And there is "order" of maturation of the soul—planes and auric layers a soul must mature into until completion/wholeness

Soul – the greater mind/being that was created by God in God's image; highly evolved truth bearing consciousness—the truth being love; created through visualization from the supreme consciousness that is itself multidimensional and infinite

Thought – energy, words, color, vibration, image, consciousness; that which is projected through frequency and through a cooperative effort between elements of orders within orders; formless consciousness that assumes form through visualization

Vibration – various levels of sound and energy; rhythmic movement

Walk-in – overshadowing; an exchange; a sharing by souls

ABOUT THE AUTHOR

LISA HROMADA is a speaker of timeless spiritual teachings and shares a simple, yet profound message: You have all that you need to create the life of your choosing. She is the author of *The Three Supreme Gifts: A Practical Approach to Self-Mastery and to Transforming Your Life Here and Now*. She brings a balanced approach to the teachings from Spirit, helping you to understand how you can create a more beneficial life here, now, and forevermore.

Website: https://www.LoveIsTheSeed.com

www.ingramcontent.com/pod-product-compliance
Lightning Source LLC
Chambersburg PA
CBHW021355090426
42742CB00009B/868